P9-EEB-242

884.2
F557

'Where Sappho Sang,

Theodore Fithian

VANTAGE PRESS
New York

WITHDRAWN

LIBRARY ST. MARY'S COLLEGE

To Cora Brooks Fithian,
my mother

FIRST EDITION

All rights reserved, including the right of
reproduction in whole or in part in any form.

Copyright © 1993 by Theodore Fithian

Published by Vantage Press, Inc.
516 West 34th Street, New York, New York 10001

Manufactured in the United States of America
ISBN: 0-533-10272-3

Library of Congress Catalog Card No.: 92-90735

0 9 8 7 6 5 4 3 2 1

$15.76 九江 6-1-94 (8w)

LIBRARY ST. MARY'S COLLEGE

To remembrance, hail!

We sit, wicked men, among pleasant things, upon a seat rock o'er-hung, thinking we see and seeing not; and the imagining of Ionia is academic in our day. But the moment may come when we recognize the face of our world, as we mould it, to be death; and we will then think no change too drastic, no renunciation too high, for the recapturing of what once demonstrated, by its actual existence, the infinite possibility in men.

—Freya Stark, Foreword to *Ionia—a Quest*

PREFACE TO YESTERDAY

"In the beginning was the Word, and the Word was with God, and the Word was God."

That obscure sentence, which opens the Gospel according to John, the beloved disciple, was originally written in Greek, as was the whole New Testament. Thus attractively attired in a euphonious language, Christianity grew up in Anatolia, the eastern hub of the mighty Roman Empire, to become the first true world religion, open to all peoples everywhere.

In the Holy Land, on the other hand, Christianity was short-lived. The leader of the faith there, James, the brother of Jesus Christ, was stoned to death by the Jews, and his church expired. Shortly thereafter, in A.D. 70, Roman legions squashed a Jewish revolt and the Jews scattered worldwide in a diaspora, not to return in sizable numbers for almost two millennia, or after World War II, fleeing the ghost of Hitler's Holocaust.

Christianity was fortunate, both in place and time, to have such a favorable birthland. Its Seven Churches of Asia, to which the New Testament was dedicated, gave it a solid foundation to overcome the many competing religions among its motley peoples. Also, being the crossroads between West and East, with easy access in all directions by either sea or land, the location was ideal for expansion. Moreover, the time was ripe. People were ready to grow spiritually to match the far-flung Roman Empire. And Greek logic demanded that any valid religion based on the worship of the Creator of the whole cosmos and everything in it had to be open to all peoples on equal terms and not be merely a tribal religion based on race, such as Judaism.

Saint Paul exemplifies such a spiritual liberation. A Jew who had bitterly persecuted the Christian upstarts, he was converted to Christ by a vision seen on the Damascus road while he was homeward bound from Jerusalem. And because he was a Roman citizen and fluent in Greek, he could travel freely and express himself to everyone. This he did vigorously and tirelessly for the rest of his life on behalf of his new faith. Some theologians call him Christianity's chief architect.

The New Testament and later the whole Bible were probably first published in Ephesus, Anatolia's leading city in the Christian era. There, legend says, some apostles foregathered after Christ's crucifixion, and Mary, his worldly mother, was brought there to spend her final days. Moreover, all essentials of publication were at hand. Papyrus rolls, the principal contemporary writing material, exported from Naucratis in Egypt, were a staple of Greek commerce. And scribes could be bought at nearby Chios's slave market, the biggest in the Aegean region. Put two hundred scribes in a well-lighted room to take dictation from a clear-speaking lector and you have Holy Scripture being mass-produced.

The Apocalypse, sometimes called Revelation, also pointed to Ephesus as the site of Holy Writ's first publication. Dictated on Patmos, the Ionian isle about sixty miles from Ephesus as a sea gull flies, this last book of the New Testament was full of dark forebodings, for Nero had been enthroned in Rome and Christians were being persecuted. They needed solace. And because the Apocalypse had many tender stanzas of comfort, it became the Bible's most quoted book, backed up by divine thunder: "I am alpha and omega, the beginning and the ending, saith the Lord."

Publication wasn't until the century following Christ's birth, however, when all of his apostles had long since gone to their rewards. Meanwhile, the Gospel was an oral tradition, part of the communal traditions that stretched back into prehistory. Fortunately, since about the ninth century B.C., that oral tradition was handled by professional Ionian bards.

Ionia was a Greek enclave on the Aegean Sea's eastern shore, its Asiatic shore. At its greatest extent, it comprised no more than a hefty slice of Anatolia's rugged littoral and its offshore islands stretching from Lesbos in the north to Rhodes. The time of its founding was auspicious. The late Bronze Age was merging into the dawning Iron Age, and mineral-rich Anatolia was the center of all the action.

The Hittites, who were master metallurgists, dominated Anatolia until about the time the Greek settlers arrived. Then they mysteriously disappeared. Before they did so, however, some stragglers seemingly passed on their metallurgical know-how to the newcomers, who were eager to learn. They left an extensive network of roads that reached into the alien, populated interior. The Greek newcomers were in a precarious position. Perilously perched on the continent's rim, they had to make themselves useful to their powerful neighbors in order to survive. So they became agents and shippers to inland royalty and privileged merchants, helping them to sell excess goods abroad and to bring them whatever overseas products they might need or want. It was a commercial relationship based on trust.

It worked beautifully. Cities went up on or near harbor facilities where they had never been built before, instead of on secure hilltops. While Athens was still a village, Ionia had great city-states, such as Ephesus; Miletus; Halicarnassus, home of Herodotus, the Father of History; Kos, home of Hippocrates, the Father of Medicine; and Samos, where Socrates once served as an ordinary soldier. To home-abiding Greeks, Anatolia was truly Sunrise Land, the land of fabled promise.

Some historians have called the city-state the best political unit ever devised by man. Composed of the orderly city itself and as much productive land adjacent thereto as was readily defensible, it was just the right size for an intimate relationship. In any case, it had whatever it takes to inspire its denizens to bring honor to their civic alter ego, rather than to themselves. For instance, trophies won in the Olympic games, begun in 776 B.C. and open to Greeks everywhere, belonged to the city-state and not to the individual.

And then there were all the other games and contests—the dance, choral singing, poetry, drama, painting, sculpture, etc.—which required long and rigorous training. From childhood on, the whole city-state was virtually a school. Everyone was helped to achieve his utmost. Small wonder, then, that ordinary city walkways, made of black and white pebbles in pleasing designs and scrubbed daily, were works of art. And that the Acropolis was an awesome symphony in marble, reaching for the stars. Striving for excellence, we all know, was a Greek motto. It says it all.

Of course there were drawbacks to giving one's total loyalty to a city-state. Should a city-state help another, even when threatened by a foreign foe? This was Ionia's gravest problem, over which not a few farsighted statesmen broke their hearts. For Ionia was held together only by common language, religion, and customs. Otherwise, city-states were fierce rivals. And this synergistic relationship accelerated their rapid advancement. Any improvement or successful innovation was quickly adopted by all.

Now we must step deeper into prehistory. For the Trojan War was an epochal event. It cannot be avoided. That ten-year-long struggle, sometimes called the first war between East and West, was fought on Anatolia's north shore, historians now tell us, to prevent the blockage, either by unacceptably high tolls or otherwise, of Greece's vital water route to the Black Sea, with its prolific grain-producing regions.

Homer, Ionia's great epic poet, however, would have no part of such matter-of-fact stuff. Instead, he related a dramatic romance. He told how Paris, prince of Troy, had abducted the beautiful wife of King Menelaus of Sparta, Helen ("the face that launched a thousand ships"), and how King Agamemnon, Achilles, Ulysses, and other heros fought gallantly for revenge and retribution. That patriotic melodrama was recited episodically by professional bards at royal courts and at all major festivals throughout the Greek world. Demand therefore was insatiable. And we, heirs of Ionia's culture, are fervently grateful that the story of human passions and failings at Troy was faithfully preserved in the oral tradition, with only minor variations.

Homer was soon followed by Hesiod, whose *Works & Days* gives us the best insight into daily life of that period, and by Sappho, popularly called "the Poetess," as Homer was called "the Poet." She sang delicately of love, the heart's unquenchable yearnings, and the loneliness of a downy bed with only moonlight for companionship. This Big Three topped scores of eloquent poets who gave the Greek language its far-out range, its flexibility, and its precision. Finally, all contributed inadvertantly to the Ionian alphabet. Later adopted by Athens, this alphabet sired all the alphabets of the Western world.

Thenceforth, the oral tradition was put into writing, but that transition stretched over a long time.

"Only the past is secure," said Daniel Webster. Said Winston Churchill, "The farther back into history we look, the farther ahead we can see."

From their earliest days, Ionians began formulating tenets of belief that made Greek culture unique, setting it apart from all others. The articles of faith were:

1. Beauty is truth.
2. Truth is man's friend.
3. The Golden Mean is the best guide to living.
4. Human talents wax best in freedom.

Behold how a Greek temple incarnates these basic principles: the quiet and lofty dignity of its fluted columns (Ionian columns), its harmonious proportions, and its airiness, flushing its sacred chambers with sunshine.

Of course those profound tenets are not discussed much nowadays, if at all. But certainly they persist, underlying and reinforcing our faith in human decency and all things good, despite no little evidence to the contrary.

Some say this is the Age of Ugliness; focus on the bad in human nature; emulate it; wallow in a sewer; be offensive, and stink to high heaven. That's smart and trendy. But surely this is a passing phase, a puerile phase, like a child's tantrum to get attention. Anyway, let's get back to Ionia.

Ionia, too, had its ups and downs as all countries have had throughout history. One of its down periods occurred during the tense years of Persian ascendancy. Then Cyrus-the-Great and Darius-the-Great, bypassing coastal Ionia, tried twice to conquer European Greece. When that puny country finally forced back the invading horde at Marathon in 490 B.C., ushering in "the Glorious Fifth Century B.C.," peace was prodigal in its blessings, but other nationalistic forces came into play.

Macedonia arose. That obscure kingdom on Greece's mountainous outskirts to the north, with its capital at Pella, suddenly loomed strong and menacing. Philip II, its hard-drinking and conquering king, was soon in a position to dictate. And Athens was again afraid.

Aristotle, who had studied at Plato's Academy in Athens for twenty-some years, was on distant Lesbos, Sappho's island, doing research in marine biology, when Philip II's envoy reached him and implored his presence in Pella to tutor the king's headstrong son. Alexander, still in his teens, had already commanded his father's decisive right wing in his last victories over the Greeks. Thus the fateful relationship between a great philosopher and a military genius began. It changed the world.

When Alexander crossed into Asia at the head of his Macedonian veterans, his army was small, his confidence reinforced by Greek culture, and his grandiose plan to conquer "the Persians on their own sandy wastes" was worked out to the smallest detail. Courage and ability, the fire to make it work, were smoldering in a heart and head jauntily wearing a white plume.

Patiently, Alexander implemented his strategy. He marched down the coast, taking all key ports beyond friendly Ionia, and refused to turn inland to fight the Persians until he had subdued Egypt, founded Alexandria on its coast, and thus fully achieved command of the sea. Then, with his lines of communication secure, he marched east.

And he often moved fast, with forced marches at night, to engage the enemy advantageously. He never lost a battle. He fought his way victoriously to the distant Indus before turning back. Eastern peoples thought he was invincible. He was a god. So his adopted Greek language naturally became the *lingua franca* of the Middle East.

Alexander-the-Great set up his world capital at Babylon (ancient Babylonia was long dead and Iraq yet unborn). There, in the fertile Land of the Two Rivers, he tried to establish the Brotherhood of Man. He took a Persian wife and urged his Macedonians to do likewise. Many did. They rebelled, however, when he tried to elevate his foreign soldiery to equal status and wages. The Macedonians demanded preferment. They wanted to remain the elite.

Alexander died a saddened man. The year was 323 B.C. He was just thirty-three years old. His soaring reputation had revived kingships in the West, where various forms of democracy, such as oligarchy, had gained the upper hand. Now, however, he considered himself a failure. But before his death, he had judiciously divided his posthumous empire among his best generals. He bequeathed Egypt to Ptolemy. Egypt was his richest, most stable, and most promising kingdom. Ptolemy was his most philhellenic general. The political marriage was happy from the start.

The Ptolemy dynasty ruled Egypt for about three hundred years. This was made possible by strictly following Pharaonic customs, such as not marrying outside the family to keep the royal blood pure. Moreover, the Ptolemies steadily improved the country's extensive infrastructure, streamlined its venerable bureaucracy, safeguarded peace with a highly mobile army, and made Egyptians richer in many ways.

Their particular pride and joy, however, was their famous library. It fervently promoted Greek culture without stint of money or effort. Functioning like a combination of the Academy and Lyceum in Athens, or a great university today, it brought the best scholars available in the Mediterranean area to Alexandria. One such was Euclid, whose *Elements of Geometry* was used as a textbook in most Western schools until recently, or for more than nineteen centuries.

The big excitement in mathematics at that time, however, was its liberation from practicality. Formerly no more than an Egyptian system of land measurement, it was now set free to roam the universe as a vehicle of thought. Distant galaxies were captured, expanding the cosmos. For now, in Alexandria, astronomy was replacing astrology.

If far-out stuff makes you dizzy, go elsewhere in this redoubtable library to fume over the hottest political issue of the day or discuss the best way to build the soaring Pharos, the granddaddy of the world's lighthouses, or join a seminar in Sappho's poetry and thus seek truth intuitively. Altogether, the university library made Alexandria the Light of the World, following Athens, which followed Ionia.

Alas, the patient work of countless generations can go up in smoke in a few days. So it was with the priceless library. A great fire consumed it, legend says, when Julius Caesar was in Alexandria dallying with the young Cleopatra, Egypt's last queen, the last enthroned Ptolemy.

Anyway, following pivotal Rome, Alexandria remains the second of three way stations back to our cultural beginnings in Ionia. And don't forget that mighty Rome was founded by Aeneas, prince of Troy, who escaped the doomed city to wander the seas and found the civic giant of the West, according to Virgil, Rome's great epic poet.

Is history, then, only random happenings connected by romance?

Mankind loves myths, but history cannot escape the inexorable law of cause and effect. What we do today, largely but not totally, makes our tomorrows.

So be young, be bold, be adventuresome. And treat yourself to a pilgrimage back to our cultural birthland.

It's really a short journey, for it's less than three thousand years ago. When measured against the billions of years of cosmic creation, that's only an eye-blink of time.

Can our Western civilization be so astonishingly young?

Our problems then and now are strikingly similar, and we seem to have been more forthright in solving them then. Early on, for instance, when foreigners made up a sizable portion of some Ionian city-states, a law was enacted to admit them to citizenship, affirming that being Greek was a matter of culture, not of race. "Know thyself," said Socrates.

Oh yes, one more thing. Regarding publication of the Bible, Johannes Gutenberg didn't invent printing with movable type until about 1450. Then his famous Bible answered a swelling demand, for more and more Christians, probably turned off by the Latinized liturgy, wanted to read the Bible themselves, free of the intercession of the clergy.

Anyway, the Reformation was in the offing, and institutionalized Christianity had demonstrated that it was not immune to human failings, such as the sale of indulgences and the infamous Inquisition, both of which were egregious.

But now it's time to shove off on your pilgrimage to Ionia. You can take this modest tome along as a guidebook. And fear not, for no Armageddon will overwhelm you en route. Happy journey!

I

This is Lesbos, the island where Sappho sang so hauntingly of love's ecstasies and pain. Here lyric poetry, which was poetry sung to the lyre, introduced love songs into the musical tradition. Sappho was their symbolic queen. To the Greek people, she was "the Poetess," as Homer was "the Poet." Aristotle called her "the Tenth Muse." And history has yet to record another poetess of comparable stature.

Sappho lived in Mytilene, the largest Greek city-state on Lesbos, the northernmost Ionian island. Ionia was a Greek enclave on the Aegean Sea's eastern shore, its Asian shore. She lived there in the latter part of the seventh century B.C., in the full flush of the Greek Renaissance and the springtime of the Western world.

Lesbos is about the same today as it was in her lifetime. It is still a silver-green island, with olive trees growing on almost every hillside; and when inland breezes blow, which is fortunately often, the tumbling leaves twinkle gaily, showing their colors fore and aft. Vineyards, too, clamber up hillsides on stone-walled terraces, and valleys are usually verdant patchworks of grain fields, pastures, and truck gardens. Elsewhere, though, Lesbos is often a shocking nakedness of rock, stark as a moonscape, for its ancient forests were felled before recorded history began, and heavy winter rains did the rest.

"More olive oil we are exporting here than any other part of Greece," I was told at Mytilene's leading export firm.

"Ten million olive trees are growing here. The oldest trees have seen eight hundred summers or more, and still producing fruit they are."

In Sappho's time, too, olives and grapes were the mainstay of Lesbian commerce. Olive oil was indispensable to cooking and feminine beauty, and wine cut the oily taste and made the heart glad. Both were in steady demand all over the Mediterranean world and were easily transportable in giant amphorae. Sappho's eldest brother, Charaxus, was engaged in the wine trade with Egypt, which annoyed her no end, for they were aristocrats and to be in trade was considered demeaning.

Nowadays tourism brings in more money than agriculture, and it has wrought many changes, including a new international life-style, wherein humans migrate seasonally like birds. Chartered planes fly directly here from northern Europe, bypassing Athens and drastically cutting airfares for Scandinavians avidly seeking sunshine after winter's long, freezing darkness. "We came to get color," a Danish girl said, and get color they do, exposing their bodies as much as fashion allows. Bare breasts are now in vogue on beaches, bravely copied by a few Greek women; but total nudity, without a loin patch to defy the sun, is usually confined to secluded coves.

The major change wrought on Lesbos by Swedes, Danes, Norwegians, and Finns, as elsewhere in Mediterranean lands, however, has been to make English the current *lingua franca*. Scandinavians have had long compulsory schooling in English, by which they can dispense with their mutually unintelligible languages. They also speak English among themselves, particularly young people, who love to throw American slang around, while their elders still prefer the Oxford accent. Anyway, Scandinavians have been the best promoters of the English language to international primacy since British

2

aristocrats first began to travel on the Continent in the grand style, setting a new fashion for the rich to follow. Ancillary thereto, they made English speech the heir presumptive to Latin, which had been heir to Greek, Sappho's deft and euphonious tongue.

"All Lesbians go to Lesbos." That graffito on an Athenian bus gains some credence by the number of females who, together or alone, come here like devout pilgrims to a shrine. Study groups, inspired by Sappho, regularly forgather here for seminars and lectures, and sometimes learned papers are written on controversial subjects of feminine interest. Their favorite rendezvous is Mithimna, also called Malivos, a medieval hill town on the north coast, hard by a fairly good beach, where steep cobblestone streets are spanned by vine-covered trellises, blessing them with shade and inviting pedestrians to loiter, to peer at stately homes half-hidden in verdure, to shop in Lilliputian stores in the business section, or to have a cool drink on a café's balcony overlooking the green-fringed sea far below.

The hill town, with its embroidery of trees and its impressive crown of medieval ruins, has a popular beach at its base. Here one can get into the inviting water after only a short, gingerly walk over tortuous stones, which children gleefully run over. Close by, under giant shade trees, is a surfside café. Here, in off hours of early morning and late afternoon, women congregate around outdoor tables for seminars and lectures and the familiar twang of the American Midwest is not infrequently heard.

"It's super," said a spectacled girl from St. Louis, lugging an armful of books. "Right now we're on women's lib movements in southern Europe. They're different from the Protestant north, ya know." The natives resent these meetings, I believe, although they are too polite to show it. They resent them as a symbol of foreign allegations of Sappho's deviant sexuality, which have been traumatic. Seizing on this sensitive point, a group of university students from Athens, male and female, avoided discussing Sappho's historical importance to rebut the foreign slander. Their attitude, I believe, merely reflects the Greek conviction that the family is socially indispensable, for without its meaningful and enduring relationships life would be emotionally arid. Ergo, any serious threat to the family is intolerable.

Sappho's sexuality has complicated local conversations to the point of blushing confusion. The word Lesbian, for instance, cannot be used to identify a native of this island, male or female, without some eyebrows going up. Plainly, deviant sexuality is something modern society feels uncomfortable with. Still, it is part of Sappho's historical mystique and cannot be ignored. It can properly be relegated to minor status, though, for Sappho's true greatness rises far above it.

The few facts we have on Sappho's life don't tell us much about her. She came from an aristocratic family, had three brothers, was possibly married to Cercolas, a wealthy man from Andros, had a darling daughter, Cleis by name, was proprietress of a girl's school in Mytilene, fell madly in love with some of her pupils, was insanely jealous when one of them left her for a rival's school, and, above all, was an incomparable poetess.

Only one of her complete poems, twenty-eight lines long, may be the sole authentic survivor. The rest are fragments. The reports that her works were collected by church authorities in 1049 and again in 1109 and publicly burned, after being officially deemed "not suitable to the temper of the time," are probably apocryphal.

Before the Christian era began, evidence strongly suggests, she was known only by quotations from other authors, a few of whom may have read the ten volumes of her collected works in Alexandria's famous library, which was totally destroyed by fire in 44 B.C. when Julius Caesar dallied there with the young Cleopatra, the last queen of Egypt.

Since then Sappho's memory has never entirely faded away. In Roman times, Ovid and Catullus revived her sensuous imagery in their poetry, and among her later devotees, Edward Gibbon, whose masterpiece, *The History of the Decline and Fall of the Roman Empire,* made him the literary idol of the eighteenth century, wrote: "In the enjoyment or neglect of our present riches we must envy the generation that could still peruse the history of Theopompus, the orations of Hyperides, the comedies of Menander, and the odes of Alcaeus and Sappho."

And in 1898 two English archaeologists, Grenfell and Hunt, retrieved a papyrus in Egypt with a poem by Sappho, or so they hopefully believed. "Still Sappho is—Sappho," said the scholarly Hunt in justification, for the lines showed unmistakably "the simple directness, the apparently effortless felicity, characteristic of the Poetess." The poem clearly deals with Sappho's vexatious brother, who was returning home from Naucratis in Egypt. Here is Hunt's unassuming translation:

Sweet Nereids, grant to me
That home unscathed my brother may return
And every end for which his soul may yearn
Accomplished see!
And thou, immortal Queen,
Blot out the past, that thus his friends may know
Joy, shame his foes—nay, rather let no foe
By us be seen!
And may he have the will
To me his sister some regard to show

To assuage the pain he brought, whose cruel blow
My soul did kill.
Yea, mine, for that ill name
Whose biting edge, to shun the festal throng,
Compelling, ceased awhile, yet back ere long
To goad us came!

Ancient Greek is such a poetic tongue, full of nature's musical sounds, that it is impossible to retain its rhythm and grace in translation, scholars say, and also its meaning. Anyway, several generations of papyrologists have fervently believed that anything written by Sappho, the queen of that musical language, is worth tracking down in dusty Egyptian temples, cold burial vaults in pyramids, or smelly piles of rubbish.

Papyrus, the Egyptian writing material used by Ionians, is perishable, particularly in damp climates. That's why it is best preserved in Egypt's dry desert air. Papyrology deals exclusively with Greek memorabilia, especially literature. Egypt is its treasure trove. For more than one thousand years Egypt was Hellenized, beginning with Naucratis, which was established by mutual agreement as an Ionian trading post on the Nile's delta, probably early in the eighth century B.C. Hellenization was intensified under the Ptolemies, who ruled Egypt for about three hundred years, spanning the formative centuries between Alexander-the-Great's death and the birth of the Roman Empire, called the Hellenistic Age. Then Alexandria, the Ptolemies' Egyptian capital, was the cultural capital of the world, following Athens, which had followed Ionia.

If Sappho's writings have mostly gone to dust, her physical likeness is preserved in many vase paintings, either surrounded by her adoring disciples, together with Alcaeus, or alone. "Softly smiling Sappho" can also be seen on not a few of Mytilene's exquisite coins, some of these possibly struck in her lifetime, but most of them afterward. These honoraria are plentiful and attest to the fact that Sappho, both during her lifetime and afterward, was virtually worshiped.

Sappho and Alcaeus! Those Lesbian poets, so often depicted together, are one of history's most enigmatic couples, held together by bonds Platonic. Both were passionately involved in politics. At the height of their careers they teamed together in a crucial election that was to be a historical turning point. It is a story bigger than both of them, wrapped in the mists of prehistory, but nonetheless discernible.

Before journeying back to Sappho's time, though, let's take our bearings. It's pleasant here on Lesbos's north coast, and evocative. You gaze out over the shimmering sea toward the Troad, the hump of Asia where the Trojan War was fought. That epochal war, sometimes called the first war between East and West, was more pivotal in history than historians yet understand. It had much to do with Ionia's beginnings and its Renaissance, and therefore with our history, too.

King Agamemnon, who led the Greeks against Troy, stopped at Lesbos and forcibly took over the island, legend says, as a staging area. Indeed, this shelving beach may have seen Greek wounded regularly brought in to recuperate and vital supplies sent out to Greek camps on Troy's coastal plain. The Trojan War lasted for ten years, so the final Greek victory must have depended on logistics as well as valor.

No archaeological digs have been made hereabouts, though, to substantiate the island's role in that war. In fact, Mithimna hasn't bothered to trace its roots further back than the medieval castle-fortress whose ruins now crown its hilltop, although it is believed to have been one of the five Lesbian city-states in Ionian times. Sappho, though, was probably never here. She was born at Eressos on the west coast, tradition says, from whence her aristocratic family moved on to

Mytilene, the present Lesbian capital. That distance is now covered in about 2.7 hours by an express bus, which slows down just enough to negotiate hairpin turns on the hilly route without even dislodging some of its sleeping passengers, who somehow manage to hold on. In Sappho's time, the sea route around the island's south coast was no doubt much easier and faster.

Mytilene, on the southeast coast facing Asia, is today a frumpy dowager town that dreams away its business hours, recalling its heyday of youthful glory only when it comes awake for the evening promenade and festal activities on the bayfront. In Sappho's time, though, this was a bustling port, always abuzz with ship-borne news from other Ionian city-states. People were eager to talk over any new trade development or the latest feminine fashion or, perhaps most of all, discuss the full portent of any fresh danger signal from Asia.

I recall an elderly Swede, a schoolteacher whom I met on my first visit to Lesbos. "For twenty years I am coming here every summer," he said. "It's nice here, isn't it? It's like home." And so began a heartwarming talk about this erstwhile Ionia, our cultural homeland, a gratifying discussion not easy to come by. It was specially good for me at the time because I had been wrestling with an old bugaboo: If Ionia is where our Western civilizations began, why has it been so long neglected by professional historians? Now, I believe, I have satisfying answers to that nagging question.

First, Philip Guedalla wasn't speaking entirely in jest when he wryly observed, "History repeats itself and historians repeat each other." Second, Ionia's dearth of source material has always kept historians from venturing into that historical limbo and still does. Third, the rise of Christianity, preaching that the Bible's Garden of Eden is the only genesis we need and backing it up with the fires of the Inquisition, made searching for our cultural roots in paganism a hazardous undertaking. Last, but certainly not least, Plato and Aristotle.

The introduction of Plato and Aristotle into medieval Europe by Arab scholars helped to ignite the Italian Renaissance, and those giant intellects became the scholastic rage all over Europe, for the Renaissance was like an unstoppable conflagration, sometimes smoldering but often raging, that spread from the Mediterranean to the North Sea. Plato and Aristotle spawned humanism, which emphasized man and his well-being here and now, rather than the church's emphasis on the life hereafter, with hell looming for miserable souls who miss out on salvation. The new faith in man himself, with its doctrine of self-help through the power of reason, bred a new enthusiasm for life. As its apostles, Plato and Aristotle were almost deified. They had organized human knowledge so beautifully and expressed it with such clarity and grace that scholars felt no need to probe into the shadowy realm of their antecedents.

The academic primacy of Plato and Aristotle, both of whom reflect Socrates' teachings, continues to this day. This is exemplified by "The Greats," the course of study at Oxford devoted exclusively to their lives and teachings. Only promising students are encouraged to take this course, the first two years of which are spent in learning the Greek language, deemed indispensable to the subject's mastery. Has "The Greats" proved worthwhile? Judging by the spectacular success of its graduates in Parliament and at 10 Downing Street, the answer is a resounding affirmative.

Sir Gilbert Murray, the late Regius Professor of Greek at Oxford, stepped beyond the confines of "The Greats" in one of his popular lectures. Extolling the cultural glories of Ionia, he cited its "new breed of men"—philosophers. Thales was the first, followed by Pythagoras, Heracleitus, and many more. And then there was Herodotus, called the Father of History only because the works of his Ionian predecessors, Cadmus and Hecataeus, were lost. And Hippocrates was the Father of Medicine, Anaximander published the first map, Hippodamus was the first city planner, etc. Sir Gilbert didn't bother to mention the most luminous Ionians of all—Homer, Hesiod, and Sappho. Everyone in the audience presumably knew them, just as they knew that Socrates, who wrote nothing himself, had been preceded by Ionia's philosophers and couldn't have escaped learning from them. Sir Gilbert finished by recounting how Miletus, in the fullness of its days as Ionia's leading city, developed a genre of gay, insouciant, and risqué stories that were blithe forerunners of Boccaccio and Rabelais.

Other scholars, such as Aldous Huxley and Stringfellow Barr, also pinpointed our cultural beginnings in Ionia, but with no follow-through. Like Sir Gilbert, they merely mention dazzling names and trail-blazing accomplishments, and let it go at that.

Well, what goes on? Isn't that a historical abortion? Isn't it sinful to send a man to the moon and yet remain almost totally ignorant of our cultural homeland on earth? Some bold historian, sometime, will come along and rescue Ionia from oblivion. Meanwhile, let us make a start.

Time and place! Those two factors make up life's corral, holding our bodies in thrall. But our minds are free to wander. So let's zero in on time. Ionia would still be lost in the Greek Dark Age if Homer hadn't brought history's light to the world. The Greek Renaissance was ignited by Homer. And Sappho, following him in about three generations with her incomparable gift of delicate poetic expression, completed the emotional stitching together of society that enabled philosophy to take root in Ionia's enriched linguistic soil, find nourishment, and develop the skill to put abstract ideas into words, and thereby to flourish. Philosophy's rationalism was Ionia's outstanding gift to the world.

Sappho, a vital link in the Greek Renaissance, is the best beacon to guide us back to our cultural beginnings. It is a journey we must make methodically, as the philosophers taught us to do, heeding, as we travel by sea and land, all headlands and landmarks, in order to observe that Ionia was in the right place at the right time to spearhead a tremendous upsurge of historical forces. In this process, Ionia was somewhat like a waterwheel that transformed the forces it received into the culture we have today.

The Aegean Sea has been justly called "the watery womb of civilization." A snug body of water between Europe and Asia, it's really a gulf of the Mediterranean, no more than two hundred miles across at its widest point and generously endowed with seductive islands. A sailor can traverse it without ever being more than forty miles from land.

A shallow sea, the Aegean smiles in summer, enjoying a wondrous clarity of light long famous with artists. In winter, though, a cold north wind is often blustery and mean and quickly kicks up watery havoc. To survive these sudden tantrums, good seamanship is indispensable, for dangerous shoals and rocks abound.

"By wind the sea is lashed to storm, but when it is unvexed, it is of all things the most amenable." Thus Solon indicated why, early on, the Aegean became the main highway between East and West. The roundabout land route between the two continents, which crossed the Hellespont (Dardanelles) where ancient Troy stood guard, was longer and more dangerous.

The large islands of Crete and Rhodes demark the Aegean Sea's southern limits, separating it from the Mediterranean proper. Rhodes is now Europe's most popular summer resort and formerly was Rome's favorite schoolhouse, where Julius Caesar and other notables studied rhetoric, and, before that, Ionia's southernmost island, with its creamy white acropolis at Lindos reaching upward like a winged prayer in marble.

Only two countries now border the Aegean Sea: Greece, a peninsula of Europe, and Turkey, a peninsula of Asia. The huge Asian peninsula was called Anatolia by the ancient Greeks, meaning Sunrise Land. It has always been a meeting place of East and West and, beneath the surface, still is. The Olympic gods had their favorite playground at Anatolia's own Mount Ida. There the fatal beauty contest between Hera, Athena, and Aphrodite took place. Paris, prince of Troy, acting as judge, awarded the coveted golden apple to Aphrodite, goddess of love. In return, she promised him the world's most beautiful woman—Helen, wife of King Menelaus of Sparta. When Paris abducted his prize, she became the "face that launched a thousand ships," according to Homer, thus starting the Trojan War.

In eastern Anatolia, Mount Ararat's snowcapped peak now looks down on Turkey's rugged frontiers with Russia, Iran, and Iraq. There, the Bible says, Noah's Ark came to rest after the great flood. Iraq was part of ancient Mesopotamia, also called the Fertile Crescent, the bounteous Land between the Rivers, where the Tigris and the Euphrates, rising in mountainous Anatolia, made the deserts bloom as they flowed to the Persian Gulf. Along their lush banks rose shining Nineveh; Babylon, with its hanging gardens; Ur; and other early centers of civilization.

The Assyrians and Babylonians, masters of the fertile lowlands south of Anatolia, came into touch with the Aegean Sea through the Hittites, who controlled the Anatolian highlands until just before the Trojan War, when they mysteriously disappeared. The Hittites were probably the first people to use iron, and they left behind a network of sturdy roads over which they had regularly traded with Assyria, Babylonia, and Egypt. They had also waged bloody wars with them. Suzerainty over the coastal lands, now known as Syria and Lebanon, was the prize usually fought for, due to their strategic value. The repeated wars, often involving thousands of chariots with slashing blades, sometimes ended in solemn nonaggression pacts, pledging eternal peace. The last surviving Hittites may have passed along their metallurgical know-how to the Lydians, who were to be Ionia's most intimate neighbors.

After the Trojan War, the victorious Greeks returned home seriously weakened by the exhausting struggle. They were soon overwhelmed by invading barbarians from the north, called Darians. Mycenae, King Agamemmon's stone-walled citadel, fell. All Greek strongholds fell. Mycenaean Greece, as historians were later to call it, ceased to exist. A Dark Age ensued, and it lasted for about four hundred years.

In those dim centuries, legend says, waves of Greeks emigrated to Ionia, starting about 1150 B.C. Initially, they may have fled from the fierce Darians, but thereafter they were steadily propelled by land hunger. Mountainous Greece is only about 10 percent arable, and primogeniture, the custom of leaving all property to the eldest son, exacerbated the dearth. And to be landless in an agricultural society is to be devoid of status.

Only younger sons emigrated. They banded together for the hazardous undertaking, bringing along all the arms they could. They expected to fight for their land and to take wives from among the natives. This was the time-honored custom. (Freya Stark, one of Ionia's closest students, has wryly pointed out that to be wives of conquerors, even of those who have slain their menfolk, has always been women's lot.)

13

As things turned out, most of the wives they took were of European stock—Phrygians, Lydians, and possibly Carians also. Their forebears migrated into Anatolia by land routes around the Black Sea, driven south, scientists say, by sunspots that periodically caused droughts, drying up the grass on the vast Eurasian steppes, forcing its nomadic tribes to seek new pastures. Those were terrible times! Forewarned by rising dust clouds of tribesmen on the march, settled communities in their path hurriedly packed and fled. Many of these European folk settled in Anatolia before the Trojan War. One of King Priam's wives was a Phrygian princess.

The Greeks were different. They came to Anatolia by sea. And the littoral they settled was mostly virgin land, for the previous invaders had settled on the lush pastures of inland plateaus. So the Greeks had to do little fighting. And the rugged coast with deep indentations of sea, so much like mainland Greece, was ideal for seafaring folk. They called their new home Ionia, after hapless Io, the nymph who fled from Zeus's amorous pursuit and was spitefully hounded on and on by Hera, Zeus's jealous wife, seeking to keep Io always beyond her husband's lustful grasp. Obviously, Ionia is a name open to different interpretations.

In its final form, Ionia comprised a sizable strip of mainland and its offshore islands stretching from Lesbos in the north to Rhodes, an island equally large, in the south. The big islands of Chios, Samos, and Kos, and hundreds of smaller ones, such as Patmos of biblical fame, were in between.

It was a cozy realm. The Greek city-states that grew up there were a quarrelsome family, fiercely independent and competitive, but held together by a common language, religion, and customs, and also by the menace of powerful neighbors who were far more culturally advanced than those they had left behind them in Europe.

Alas, our traditional perception of Ionia, derived exclusively from academe, is quite different. It is really a ludicrous nonperception—a vague place, sort of nameless, almost totally unknown, and insignificant. Modern scholars, reflecting the Plato-Aristotle syndrome, have ignored all preceding history except for Homer. Public demand for his masterpieces, the *Iliad* and *Odyssey,* was insatiable. They were translated into all major languages and taught in schools of most countries of the Western world for countless generations.

To translate Homer as faithfully as possible, scholars became obsessed with Ionia's dialects, for his works were composed in two of the three dialects spoken there. Incidentally, this philological focus had its lighter side. Scholars turned into linguistic detectives. Where was Homer born? Seven Greek cities claimed Homer as a native son. Inasmuch as both Ionian and Aeolian dialects were used in his epics, although principally the former, scholars limited his probable birthplace to two cities on the dialectal borderline: Smyrna and Chios. Additional internal evidence gave the final nod to Chios.

For scholars, that was a felicitous triumph. Unfortunately, those dialects became a scholastic fixation, branding Ionia with an exaggerated divisiveness, to wit: in the north, on Lesbos and the opposite littoral, were the Aeolians, Sappho's kin, who spoke the soft, dulcet patois of eastern Greece, from whence they had emigrated. Central Ionia, which includes offshore Chios and Samos, was inhabited by true Ionians, who came from Athens and its surrounding countryside and spoke the Attic dialect. Darians, the last to emigrate, settled southern Ionia and spoke a harsher tongue, which they had acquired in the Peloponnisos, the southern part of the Greek peninsula where they had eventually made their home. There, over the centuries, they had been thoroughly Hellenized, like all invading barbarians before them. Barbarians—that is what the Greeks called anybody who didn't speak their language.

Although the foregoing was true enough, the false linguistic emphasis trivialized history and grossly distorted it by depicting Ionians as three separate peoples. In reality, the Ionians were more unified than mainland Greeks, as the Peloponnesian War was to prove. Nevertheless, in academe's view, aside from Ionia's dialectical divisions, the place held little importance. Scholarship, like all human activities, has its sins, both of commission and omission.

What has happened to curiosity—a quality that characterized the Ionians? Has it vanished from the classical departments of our universities? For instance, classicists have made scant effort to explain how Athens's "glorious fifth century" came about. Did it spring out of nothing? Or did it naturally evolve from Ionia's "burgeoning sixth century," which culminated the volcanic creativeness that began with the Greek Renaissance? That's Ionia's big story. So, as we travel back to our cultural homeland, we must ask ourselves how its exceptional creativeness came about.

To begin with, Ionians lived with danger. Perched precariously on the fringe of Asia and hopelessly outnumbered in manpower by the mighty kingdoms on their borders and in the vast hinterland beyond, the Ionians realized they were in constant jeopardy. This sense of peril kept them alert and forever trying to improve, in one way or another, their vulnerable position. Tranquillity is soporific, detrimental to creativity. This was plainly demonstrated in the Roman Empire's "Long Peace."

Let's take a quick look at the more than three hundred peaceful years that began with Augustus, the first Roman emperor. Then peripheral wars were more like police actions and monumental achievements, such as far-flung roads, bridges, harbors, aqueducts, coliseums, triumphal arcs, military outposts, and guardian walls against invasion, built up the empire's infrastructure. Its motley population, composed of many races, enjoyed a stable social order with codified laws. And because Romans had inherited the Greek veneration of law, to some extent at least, the laws were called "majestic." Some Roman lawyers, such as Cicero, are still considered models of professional competence and men of high principle. Nonetheless, those peaceful centuries were culturally sterile. Nothing really new was produced. The practical Romans had a genius as organizers, administrators, and builders. They were content with their inherited Greek culture; it gave them a solid foundation for all they wanted to do and inspired them to do it.

The mighty Roman Empire, master of the world, was a major culmination in the cultural continuum that began in Ionia and has never really stopped. That vital linkage is best exemplified by Virgil (70–19 B.C.), Rome's greatest poet, who inspiringly appeared just as the Roman Republic, torn by civil war, was about to be transformed into the Roman Empire.

Virgil's beloved masterpiece, the *Aeneid,* was straight out of Homer. It relates how Aeneas, prince of Troy, escaped from the doomed city and, after a long, adventure-packed voyage to Latium, heroically led the struggle to found the Eternal City on the Tiber. Its gospel was simple: adventure can be richly rewarding. That clearly supported the empire's advocates, led by the redoubtable Julius Caesar until felled by his assassin's daggers. The Roman Senate, which feared the concentration of power in one man, led the formidable opposition.

The early Roman emperors had a single imperial goal—peace. Every Roman desperately wanted an end to strife, particularly the internecine strife that had been the empire's birth pangs. So strong barbarian tribes in northern

Briton, north of the Rhine, north and east of the Danube, and in Anatolia's Parthia, who repeatedly tried to break into the Pax Romana's orderly confines, were systematically repelled.

Roman citizens had security and peace. They could freely choose their vocations, travel anywhere in the civilized world, prosper according to their worth, indulge in prosperity's vices, and build nobly on their Greek culture.

In contrast, Ionians started from scratch. They were newcomers to a vast continent. Their neighbors were powerful and warlike. Ionians lived in peril. And their abiding sense of danger was a constant spur to their creativity.

Before we go further, we must face up to an awkward question about Ionia's beginnings around 1150 B.C. How could young Greek males come to Anatolia, take alien wives, and impose the culture of their abandoned homeland upon their new families? In no way could this have been done, I believe, if it were not for the institution of slavery.

All Mediterranean peoples had slaves. Slaves were a continuous harvest of the incessant wars and always profitable. No one doubted slavery's legitimacy, not the early philosophers, not the Christians when they came. Saint Paul, as the Bible relates, advised slaves to obey their worldly masters, promising only spiritual equality to everyone—Greek and Jew, male and female, slave and freeman—in Christ our Lord. Slavery was to endure in the Western world for more than two thousand years, until a bloody civil war eradicated its last stronghold in the United States of America.

With Greeks, slaves were usually female domestics. When Greek warriors sacked a city, all males were slain and only healthy women and children were taken captive. In Homer's *Iliad*, one of the most touching scenes occurred when Hector, before going out to fight Achilles, took leave of his wife, Andromache, and their young son. He knew Troy was doomed if he was slain, and he dreaded the thought of his beloved wife and son as Greek slaves.

The most intelligent female slave, particularly if she was Greek, usually taught her master's children. In that high post, she was like a member of the family, and the relationship was sometimes deeply affectionate. Boys, when about eight years old, were put under the instruction of a man, usually a slave also, who taught them how to draw a bow, swordplay, horsemanship—all the manly arts. In any case, teachers were beholden to the master of the house. Custom decreed decent treatment for all slaves, but their master still held the power of life and death over them. Thus education, like everything else, was a male prerogative, and the Greek pioneers in Ionia, feeling their authority challenged in the new environment, probably imposed an indoctrination of Greek customs upon their new families, thoroughly and unsparingly. And because similar traditions of slavery and of male authority were shared by their native wives, husbands had no real marital opposition.

And so the Asiatic Greeks built themselves great cities, and it was a labor of love. Each city's site and architecture grew out of leaping camp fires around which Ionians talked while temporarily bivouacked, for gardens, orchards, and pastures for livestock had to come first. And then stone by huge stone, meticulously fitted together, the fortress-home went up, scowling upon the outside world. Inside was a harmonious arrangement of mosaic walkways, noble statuary, and all civic amenities, including public toilets. Individual homes were suitably clustered on the outskirts, like grapes on the vine, but not too dense. On the highest elevation was an acropolis, the polished marble of its temples supremely lustrous, offering a bouquet of beauty to the gods.

The city's stout walls might also protect its vital harbor and quays, and if fortune smiled, its surrounding countryside would be large and fertile enough to provide, in normal times, all of life's necessities, including playgrounds for games and festivals and somewhere a lonely meadow of dreams, where a troubled spirit could find the balm of solitude. This was important in city-states, which were not totally unlike beehives.

Building each city took generations, and it was a long, hard lesson in democracy. Only democracy could generate the social power to enable a few people to accomplish so much. Slave labor was always involved, but it was probably only a minority. Artisans and other working citizens were also warriors, ready to seize their weapons when alarms sounded, for all men had to serve in the militia until age sixty-five. Thus the meticulous city builders, working in stone, wood, and metals, began father-and-son relationships and guild relationships that possibly developed the best masons, architects, and sculptors that the world had known.

The city-state was the only political unit in Ionia. No other existed. It was home, fatherland, and sacred temple rolled into one. Ionians gave it their total allegiance. And it was exactly the right size, seemingly, to fit the human heart. Everyone found some niche in it and filled it proudly. Citizens did their utmost to bring honor to the city and thereby to themselves. A prize won in the Olympic games, for instance, in another athletic contest, or in music, dancing, or painting contests, belonged temporarily to the city, to be passed on to the next victorious city; it never belonged to the individual who had won it.

According to Aristotle, "The city-state came into existence out of necessity, and continued to function for the sake of the good life." Some scholars say it was the best political unit ever devised by man. By inspiring its citizens to make the most of their talents, and giving them an opportunity to

20

do so, from creating exquisite black-and-white pebble walkways, to winning a choral contest, to designing a magnificent temple, the city-state was a prime factor in Ionia's creativity.

The most surprising thing about these city-states was their locations. That was something new. Heretofore, security had been the city-states' overriding consideration. Mycenae and other hilltop strongholds of ancient Greece make this clear; also the royal capitals of contemporary kingdoms, such as Egypt's Memphis and Persia's Susa, were located deep within each country, insulated by hundreds of leagues of desert wastelands. Ionia's city-states, however, ignored geographical security. With few exceptions, they were sited primarily for commerce; hence they were topographically open and exposed. In this respect, they were probably the first of their kind.

Miletus, Ionia's largest and most progressive city, was typical. It rose resplendently from the flat estuary of the Meanders River. Its city walls encompassed four good harbors, two of them connected by a canal; otherwise, the city was pitifully vulnerable. Orchards and farms occupied the flat land around it for miles and miles. And this fertile Meanders valley, which provided easy access to the interior highlands, was thus a main highway of commerce. It also made it easy for hostile armies to assault Miletus and to live off the fat countryside during a long siege. This happened several times, disastrously. It was a risk the city's founders had been fully aware of, and they had accepted it.

Thereby hangs one of history's most fateful decisions. Miletus was to suffer much for its boldness and pride. But also, as if fulfilling an ambiguous prophecy of Didyma's oracle, it became the first world-class city. As such, it left a generous legacy that few other cities, if any, have equaled. This happened when Athens was still a village.

21

Man for man, Ionian warriors were considered the best in Asia. Foreign monarchs eagerly sought their services as mercenaries. And "second sons," the dispossessed victims of primogeniture, of which an Ionian family might have many, found soldiering abroad an adventurous career. It was also a good way to earn a stake to start out in business back home, if they got back home. Ionian warriors served all over the Near East. Far up the Nile in Egypt, Greek mercenaries carved graffiti on a monolith, recording their presence in that god-forsaken desert. And later Xenophon, the famous pupil of Socrates, soldier, and author, related the long march home of ten thousand Greek mercenaries out of their Mesopotamian entrapment, recording a duplication of what some Ionian mercenaries, either individually or in groups, had no doubt experienced aforetime.

Early on, Ionians faced up to their dire predicament. Because it was hopeless to fight a brave foe that might outnumber them fifty to one, their survival depended on safeguarding peace. Each city-state made its deliberations separately. But the harsh facts of geography and the tremendous differences in manpower could not be altered. On the other hand, the fruits of friendship appeared to be exceptionally promising. The economies of the seafaring Greeks and of their land-locked neighbors neatly meshed; they were complementary, going together like bread and butter. It was an ideal set-up for a mutually beneficial relationship. As a result, each Ionian city-state adopted the same strategy, with only minor variations.

First, diplomats abroad would assiduously cultivate good relations and would forewarn of any unfavorable political shift; second, a strong sword arm to make an assault extremely costly would discourage random attacks; third, and most important, Ionians would make themselves economically indispensable to their powerful neighbors and, as far as humanly possible, to all potential foes that loomed beyond.

With their vivid imaginations and rhetorical gifts, Ionians must have discussed the obvious facts of their perilous situation endlessly, but the magnitude of the potential trade between Asia and the whole Mediterranean basin was beyond the wildest calculations of any man alive. Ionians only knew that serving their neighbors well as shippers, merchants, agents, and commercial advisers was more than profitable; it was their security, their family's lives. Only that compelling consideration would induce them to abandon tradition and to build an exposed city to serve commerce, like a prostrate slave, with only a stout wall to safeguard its reckless vulnerability.

In contrast, Miletus's chief foreign rival, Tyre, Phoenicia's leading seaport, was a bastion of strength. Built on a tiny island, its high walls rose directly from the water. Alexander-the-Great, after he had established his Anatolian headquarters for the conquest of Asia in 334 B.C., swept down the coast in the initial phase of his gigantic undertaking. His purpose was to bring all of Asia's Mediterranean seaports under his authority. Persia had to be denied access to the Middle Sea (Mediterranean). This would keep his maritime line of supply secure and also prevent an enemy force from being built up in his rear, for Persian machinations were endless. Only then could he safely turn inland to engage the vast armies of the King of Kings. When Tyre refused to submit to his generous terms, however, he had to invest it. Many months were required for his troops, and many thousands of conscript laborers, working day and night, to build a mole to the island in order to breach the city's stout walls. It was Alexander's worst hang-up, and he chafed at the unexpected delay.

Miletus was probably the first true river seaport. Huge stones had to be barged downriver to make a foundation in soggy ground. Nevertheless, it was soon a thriving city, with manufacturing as well as foreign trade. To feed its two main industries, textiles and furniture, bales of raw wool and rafts of timber came down the Meanders from upland meadows and hillside forests that were ever receding, causing erosion that eventually silted up the river and doomed the city. But for more than a millennium the West's first metropolis continued to shine from the richest shore in the Mediterranean, like a civic beacon, metaphorically saying, "Behold the Ionians! The sea is their pasture."

Miletus was famous for its fine woolens. Sappho probably wore them as chitons and tunics. Perhaps she also reclined on a graceful divan from Miletus and lifted a chalice from one of its tripod tables in order to drink the customary cool, diluted wine. Perhaps, too, the divan looked luxuriant because its soft sheepskin covering was a beautiful purple, made from Phoenicia's secret dye, a precious color that, later on, Roman Caesars restricted to royalty. This widely coveted dye, in fact, gave Phoenicia its Ionian name: *phoenix* is Greek for "purple." Extracted from Phoenicia's murex shellfish, the dye was that country's most valuable export.

The Meanders River gave us the English word *meander,* meaning "to wander aimlessly." The river was erratic, always changing course, and heavy winter rains made it rambunctious. When it washed away valuable farmland, as it often did, irate farmers sued it at law. The river was rich. Legal judgments against it were paid from tolls collected from scores of ferries, barges, and big ships that were constantly using its docks.

The wealth of Miletus, though, was merely the wherewithal for a greater contribution—philosophy. Material prosperity gave men the means to be impractical, to think of abstract things. Thales, the first philosopher, was born in Miletus either in Sappho's lifetime or shortly thereafter. He was a legendary figure. Many stories were told about him! "He was walking along at night and fell into a well, because he was always looking at the stars," a wine-shop waitress said. An old vintner muttered this story: "After the disastrous harvests of several years ago, the weather showed signs of changing. Thales leased all the olive presses available, then leased them out himself when the rains came. He made a killing." "He was always figuring things out with numbers," an admiring student said. "He foretold that eclipse of the sun that occurred when the Medes and Persians were locked in battle up in the highlands [May 28, 585 B.C.]. And the soldiers stopped fighting when day changed into night and fled in panic."

Thales grew up on poetic riches. Starting with Homer's martial beat and then taking wing in lyrical flights, riding emotion into beauty, he explored reaches of imagination, or of reality, far beyond ordinary mortals. Only thus could the Greek language have acquired the range and flexibility to embody new concepts and to express them with precision and clarity. Miletus, inheriting Ionia's outpouring of poetry, primarily from Mytilene, became Ionia's cultural leader with the rise of philosophy, following the great days of Sappho and Alcaeus and lyrical singing.

Philosophy, called the mother of all the sciences, really started out as a science itself. Thales was not concerned with questions of ethics, aesthetics, or man's relationship to God. He wanted to discover the ultimate nature of matter, down to the last irreducible particle, out of which the whole physical universe was created. So the atom (that which cannot be cut) was postulated. Miletus's school of philosophy was probably responsible therefore, but Leucippus of Miletus in the fifth century B.C., and his famous pupil Democritus of Abdera, were its principle elaborators.

Not until modern times, however, was the atom believed to be a miniature universe with tremendous power. Splitting it would release that power, some scientists believed. Pres. Franklin D. Roosevelt was persuaded this could be done. The result was the atomic bomb and Hiroshima and Nagasaki and the end of World War II in the Pacific arena.

Ionian philosophy had started out as a science, but the emphasis soon shifted to rationalism. The methodology of human reasoning was, to Ionian philosophers, their abiding mainstay. It was their faith. And that faith was strong. Reason was held to be man's most reliable guide in life; it could make the best decisions regarding man's welfare on earth, and perhaps, because it was God-given, it might also be the best guide to any future life. Reason exalted man into the outcourts of divinity but stopped short there. In any case, Ionian minds were captivated by it. Rationalism became a conscious part of their lives and thenceforth an enduring pillar of Western civilization.

Rationalism functions as part of man's higher nature, his spiritual nature; it struggles relentlessly with his tribal and religious prejudices and with all the dark passions that haunt his soul. Plutarch (A.D. 46–120) has given us a good portrait of man's lower nature, his physical or satanic nature: "If you will scrutinize and open up yourself you will find a storehouse of evils and maladies, not entering from abroad, but home-bred, springing from vice, plenteous in passions. Wickedness frames the engines of her own torment. She is a wonderful artisan of a miserable life."

The subjective struggle between man's good and evil natures is a continuing one, as is the struggle between their overt manifestations in society. Even after Christianity joined rationalism as a second pillar of Western society, supplanting previous religious beliefs, society was sustained in equilibrium by the tension between the two—an equilibrium never entirely still and sometimes rocking to extremes. It is rational-ism, as a rule, that curtails man's worst excesses of tribal and religious fanaticism.

This social flux, by the way, is a fulfillment of Heraclei-tus's postulated "universal flux," brought about by the tension between opposites, such as the positive and negative poles of electricity. Hegel and Marx later took up this philosophy and elaborated on it. And because one of its manifestations, the class struggle, as interpreted by Marx, was considered pivotal in history by the Kremlin's theorists, Heracleitus's phi-losophy, or rather a distortion thereof, played a stellar role in modern affairs until very recently.

"Life is short and art is long, experiments dangerous, deductions difficult, and conclusions uncertain." Hippocra-tes, the Father of Medicine, could not have written those words if he hadn't absorbed the teachings of the nearby Mile-sian philosophers. Indeed, he was their ardent disciple. On his native Kos, he worked tirelessly to remove the practice of medicine from the witchcraft of Aesculapius's priests, as superior as that diverse practice was to medicine's primitive state elsewhere. Hippocrates wanted medicine based on an enduring scientific foundation, and he spent his life building up that foundation of patiently assembled and analyzed case histories and their best cures. He also gave the medical profes-sion a moral code. His Hippocratic Oath, still administered to graduating medical students, holds physicians to a high, uncompromising standard of professional conduct. They are strictly enjoined never to take advantage of their intimate relations with patients in any way. To succeed in medicine, Hippocrates declared, a man must love the art, and to love the art he must first love his fellowman, for the one is impossible without the other.

The Milesian School of Philosophy also created a new type of woman—the hetaera. They were paramours of a better class, valued more for their intelligence and social graces than for their physical attractiveness. Students of philosophy, like male students everywhere, wanted female companions for their evening celebrations. And this included, oddly enough, intelligent talk. Free-flowing wine and lusty drinking songs were mainstays of festive evenings, but intelligent talk was radically new, like philosophy itself. Of course the more physical beauty a girl possessed, the better, but a ready wit was indispensable. The lively and witty students set a trend. Soon the town's businesspeople followed suit. Evening banquets featuring lighthearted speeches and interesting conversation became the new mode. Professional entertainers, singers, dancers, and acrobats were kept in the background, with only occasional appearances. Hetaerae were the new queens of the evening. They were in constant demand.

Aspasia was such a party girl. And she elevated the new female genre to the pinnacle of society. Leaving Miletus for Athens, she became the beloved consort of Pericles, the adroit and strong-willed Athenian ruler in "the glorious fifth century B.C." Her salon was famous. And she graciously presided over official banquets, soothing piqued egos with charm, drawing guests out to exhibit their best talents, and making the evening sparkle with spontaneity.

Aspasia also wrote important official speeches for Pericles and other civic bigwigs. She had the gift of expression and the rare skill of discerning how people really felt. Socrates repeatedly paid her public tribute, warmly complimenting her for graciousness and wit. And Pericles, in his famous Farewell Address, called himself the most fortunate of all living men because "Athens has confined her glory and Aspasia her happiness to me."

28

In retrospect, though, this was the age of Socrates. He is the person people remember as the greatest philosopher. Plato extolled his beloved teacher in his voluminous writings, and Aristotle, who was a student at Plato's Academy for twenty years, also acknowledged Socrates' inspiring leadership.

Socrates was the best fruit of Ionia's philosophy; he exemplified man's victory over himself. A squattish man, rather ugly, he still served as an ordinary soldier when he was forty years old. "An unexamined life is not worth living," he said. So he examined himself, and continually did repair work on an unsatisfactory psyche. He jokingly withstood the worst rigors of wintertime military duty; he put up with constant carping by an ill-tempered wife; he enjoyed conviviality with free-flowing wine, or all-night conviviality without it. To him, intelligent talk to illuminate a troublesome aspect of life, and thereby to make one of life's burdens less heavy, was the best pastime. He prized a thirst for truth in a student or companion, but goodwill was indispensable. Goodness, he believed, is present for everyone to harvest. And goodness is invincible.

Socrates taught philosophy for free to anyone who would listen; he lived his philosophy, but he didn't preach it. And because the year was 399 B.C. and Athens still wallowed in low morale, having lost the Peloponnesian War five years before, its improvised government of Thirty Tyrants, seeking a scapegoat for their endless frustration, condemned Socrates to death for corrupting the young.

Athens thereby violated for the first time its long-standing policy of freedom of speech. That freedom had been punctiliously observed through three stressful decades of war, but now, in its gloomy aftermath, freedom was gravely wounded in the one public figure who had refused to be gloomy.

When his friends visited Socrates in prison for the last time, they begged him to flee Athens, according to the arrangements they had already made. He declined. He was a citizen of Athens, he reminded them gently, and good citizens obey the laws. As he raised his cup of hemlock to drink, he said, "Please remember, dear friends, you won't be burying Socrates; you'll only be burying this old body." So he drank, and before darkness engulfed him he managed to console his friends again, saying, "Of this you may be sure, dear friends: no real harm can come to a good man either in this life or after death."

At a point on the mainland about midway between Lesbos and Chios another river, the Hermus, runs inland from the Aegean Sea to the interior highlands. This provides the second easy route between the coast and the vast hinterland. Cyme is a busy little port near the Hermus's mouth. Here Hesiod was born.

With Homer born on Chios and Sappho on Lesbos, that means the Greek Renaissance's three leading protagonists had native city-states almost in sight of each other, Cyme on the mainland and Lesbos and Chios offshore, forming a triangle pointing east. The three ports are only a few hours apart by ship. This epitomizes Ionia's snugness and the rich diversity therein.

Homer lived about four hundred years after the Trojan War. Looking back on the superb Greek warriors and masterful kings who had fought in that war, he winnowed folklore to portray, in the *Iliad* (Troy was also called Ilium), their climactic victory. In a sequel, the *Odyssey,* he related the strange adventures that befell one of the war's heroes, Odysseus, on his long voyage home to his island kingdom, Ithaca. His happy reunion with his faithful wife, Penelope, eventually was made complete by disposing of her forty importunate suitors.

Homer composed his epics for recitation in Ionia's aristocratic courts, but they were also regularly recited at major festivals by popular demand. The common people, too, considered themselves heirs to Troy's conquerors. This gave them a proud sense of identity and inspired them to emulate their heroic ancestors. These emotional kindlings swiftly grew into a boundless spiritual conflagration—the Greek Renaissance, which quickly spread from Ionia to all Greeks throughout the Aegean region.

Thus the long Dark Age came to an end. Light broke upon the world. Our history began.

Generated by many minds awakened and inspired, the Renaissance developed its own momentum. Outstanding in the popular upsurge was Homer's junior contemporary, Hesiod. He was atypically Greek. He hated the sea. When his seafaring father inherited the family farm back in Boeotia, they returned to mainland Greece. There Hesiod embarked upon farming life, interspersed with flights of his poetic genius. His two major works, *Works & Days*, a chronicle of farm life, and *Theogony*, a genealogy of the Olympic gods, were, in a sense, siblings. Hesiod, often toiling from dawn to dark to earn his daily bread, was preoccupied with the fickle weather, because it ordains a farmer's fate. Weather, it seems, is the favorite toy of the capricious gods.

Works & Days gives us the best close-up of daily life in antiquity. In it, Hesiod scolds his brother for greed and laziness, condemns the petty bureaucrats as insatiable "eaters of bribes," praises the virtues of industry and honesty as indispensable to success, gives practical advice on seasonal chores, and laments that human beings are not selectively bred, as horses, cattle, sheep, hogs, goats, and dogs are successfully bred to improve the species. Man cannot be master

31

of his fate, Hesiod complains, as long as he breeds children at hazard.

Hesiod composed his *Theogony* first, and this elevated him in public opinion to rank with Homer as a chief architect of the Olympic family of gods. In this respect, Homer and Hesiod merely popularized certain aspects of Ionian folklore and perhaps added a few deft touches to sharpen divine personalities. In any case, Xenophanes of Colophon accused them of ascribing to the gods all that is shameful in human conduct—adultery, thievery, deceit of all kinds. He also accused them of shameful anthropomorphism, that is, of creating gods in their own image, saying: "Yea, and if oxen and lions and horses had hands, and could paint with their hands, and produce works of art, as men do, horses would paint the form of gods like horses, and oxen like oxen, and make their bodies in the images of their several kinds. . . ."

Anthropomorphism, of course, was and is worldwide. People can only think in forms and symbols they know. And so began the Greek cult of the body. For it was the form divine, possessed by gods and goddesses who enjoyed eternal youth, free of worldly cares and free of the cruel ravages of time. Beauty was the highest good. And beauty and goodness were identical. Thus preached Greek painters and sculptors with their hands. Their gods were powerful and majestic, and beautiful in their nakedness. But females, custom decreed, had to be clothed. This was a boon to art. Greek artists learned how to handle draperies with consummate skill, rendering folds either for diversity, coverage, or flow, so that one could almost see the material ripple, like wind-blown hair, clinging to the body, enhancing its graceful symmetry.

The Olympic family of gods was not morally superior to humans. Homer and Hesiod's theology has been stoutly defended by not a few scholars on the grounds of its honesty.

Their gods are also part of a universe in which evil abounds and reflect that reality. At least, their theology avoids the Christian ambiguity of an All-Wise, All-Powerful, and All-Merciful God ruling a universe rife with suffering, injustice, and sin.

The Olympic divinities were an Ionian masterpiece. Many were of Asiatic origin. Apollo, the most Greek of all the gods, fought for Troy, as Homer relates. The most promising gods and goddesses encountered by Ionians in Anatolia were adopted by them, Sir Gilbert Murray points out, shriven of their grotesque and primitive aspects and polished into widespread social acceptability. This was accomplished principally at festivals. There bards and priests, presenting gods in stories and on occasions of worship, would gradually modify them to accord with human preferences. Finally, after countless centuries, the Olympic family was brought into being. It peoples our sky today. Stars and planets and constellations are their namesakes. Indeed, all planets, save Earth, bear their Latinized names—Mercury, Venus, Mars, Jupiter, etc. Even the American rocket that first took man to the moon adhered to the classical tradition. It was named *Apollo.*

To Ionians, all nature was a divine manifestation. That made their religion very intimate. Every mountain, brook, and tree was invested with its own deity, giving their physical surroundings a spiritual dimension. Things seen were animated by things unseen. Hence all nature called for reverence. Domiciles, too, had their household gods. So religion and man had a constant companionship. Sometimes this was frightening, sometimes inspiring, but usually just comforting. Gods and men, the Ionians believed, were related. They somehow belonged together. Thus myths were born, and a godhead created in man's best image.

The instinctive process of religious creation continues. Many Christians, for instance, no longer believed in an Old

Testament God that is jealous and vengeful and demands human sacrifice, such as the life of a firstborn son. We cannot worship a god with attributes we condemn in ourselves. And it is only in modern times that Mary, the mother of Jesus, who with her accessibility, gentleness, and mercy, appeared to be humanity's best friend, was elevated to heaven's zenith as Mary, the Mother of God.

The Hermus River, flowing inland just north of the inlet to Smyrna, was considered the dividing line between the Aeolian and Ionian dialects. And like the Meanders River, it played a leading role in Ionia's rise to primacy in the West. Not far inland, the Hermus abruptly curves south, flowing out of Phrygia, or erstwhile Phrygia, into Lydia. There it flowed past Sardis, with its grandiose acropolis on Mount Tmolus, an architectural crown combining Ionian culture and Lydian wealth. Caravans from Assyria and Babylonia would pause here, dispose of some of their merchandise, and then continue to Cyme. There the remaining cargo, which was usually foodstuffs and household luxuries, was shipped to Ionian city-states and elsewhere overseas. And down the Hermus valley Phrygian elegies would gaily tumble and leap the narrow channel to Lesbos.

Phrygia is a fabled land. It was the first kingdom to gain Anatolian dominance after the Hittite collapse. King Midas brought it early fame. His fabulous gold and silver mines near Gordium, his royal capital, made him the world's richest man. He wasn't satisfied, though. He wanted more. And because he had once come to the aid of a sorely hurt satyr, Dionysus, Lord of Satyrs and God of Wine and of Wild Mountain Music, wanted to repay his kindness. So Dionysus asked the unhappy king what he desired. The king wanted everything he touched turned to gold. Granted! Then when the king tried to eat, he

34

realized his suicidal mistake, gasping in horror. Dionysus took pity on him and made him normal again. But the legend of "the Midas touch" lingers on.

The king was very human. He made another serious mistake. Presuming to judge a music contest between Apollo and Pan, he awarded the prize to Pan. Promptly Apollo turned Midas's ears into those of an ass. The king was mortified and tried to hide his shame. Only his barber knew, and he fearfully buried the secret in a hole in the ground. Reeds that grew up whispered the secret to the breeze, and the breeze told everyone. Those Phrygian reeds, as we shall see, were something special.

What goes on here? Those myths may have been Phrygian originally, but Greek gods are involved and they are part of Ionian folklore. In truth, that is the way things were. Ionia was, for the West, antiquity's mouthpiece. It was our sole channel to prehistory. Ionia's oral tradition was the only one to come down to the Western world. Homer exemplified this, winnowing Ionia's rich folklore to tell us about the Trojan War, Mycenaean Greece, and King Priam's many allies among Ionia's Asiatic neighbors. Outside of that folklore, the West knew nothing. Whatever culture we derived from elsewhere was filtered to us through Ionians and transmuted by them in the process. This formula was drastically altered only by archaeology. That didn't come along, meaningfully, until the nineteenth century. Then it was too late to have any effect on our culture, which had already been set in an Ionian pattern.

How we see things through Ionian eyes is exemplified by Persia. That name is derived from Persis, the Ionian name for the high eastern plateau beyond Anatolia. The natives called their country Iran, meaning Land of the Aryans. This name didn't come into general usage, however, until after

World War II. Then a worldwide outbreak of nationalistic fervor, particularly among stateless people demanding their own homeland, caused much local agitation and instability, an abrasive state of affairs still going on in more than a few places, such as Ireland, Sri Lanka, and Palestine.

We tend to forget that archaeology is almost wholly confined to the last two centuries. This confuses our thinking. Heinrich Schliemann, the brilliant German businessman and avid student of Homer, for instance, was a modern man. He took part in the California Gold Rush of 1849 and became an American citizen. His preoccupation with Homer's stories, though, wouldn't allow him to rest. He used his wealth to startle the world in 1867 by discovering Troy, which most scholars had believed to be mythical. He followed this up by excavating Mycenae, with its surprising wealth of artifacts, including a golden death mask that he attributed to King Agamemnon. The world at large was pleased by this vindication of Homer's supposedly romantic history and astonished by the riches of ancient kings. As a result, public enthusiasm was engendered for digging up the wonders of the past.

Archaeology became scientific and painstaking. In due time, it unearthed more wonders. Knossos, for instance, was discovered by Sir Arthur Evans and publicized by him in 1900 as "the oldest civilization of the Mediterranean world." This, too, was confusing. We automatically pinned Knossos on our genealogical tree. Although Sir Arthur had clearly established its seniority to other Western societies, he had failed to make the public realize that Knossos had been interred in history's graveyard either before or during Greece's Dark Age; hence it could have had no direct influence on the West. Indirectly, though, Cretan influence probably came down to us through Ionia. Enough Cretan artifacts have been found on Kos and Rhodes to indicate that Ionia was the meeting ground of Asiatic and Mediterranean peoples before Mycenaean Greeks had settled there. Indeed, Crete's famed double-headed ax is believed to be of Anatolian origin.

In a way, it's a pity that we're not the cultural heirs of Knossos. Then we might have inherited the thrilling sport of bull leaping. That was Crete's favorite sport, as numerous wall paintings in Knossos attest. They vividly depict young athletes, male and female, grabbing a charging bull by the horns, nimbly somersaulting over its back, and landing gracefully on their feet. As a spectacle, bull leaping must have been breathtaking, exhibiting superb timing, fluid grace, and blithe indifference to death.

Great wealth, history tells us, is not always a boon. At least, Phrygia's golden riches were its undoing. About 700 B.C., Phrygia was attacked by a new wave of barbarians from the north, called Cimmerians. Lydia, finally fearful for its own safety, went to its neighbor's faltering defense. Their joint forces, under Lydia's King Gyges, finally prevailed. Then wily old Gyges turned on his stricken neighbor, administered a knockout blow, and took over the rich kingdom, adding its gold and silver mines to his own. Thus Gyges's great-grand-son, King Croesus, who reigned from 560 to 546 B.C., was, in his turn, hailed "the world's richest man," like King Midas had been before him. "As rich as Croesus" is still a current phrase.

Legends can be powerful. Alexander-the-Great knew this, and he was wise enough to use them. In selecting Gordium, the old Phrygian capital, to be headquarters for his projected conquest of Asia, he got a mountain-girt stronghold in a strategic location for a base depot, an inland anchor to protect his land route to Europe, and the opportunity to be proclaimed, prophetically, the master of Asia.

Gordius, the peasant father of King Midas, who was called to the throne of Phrygia from his plow, tied his farm wagon to a pillar in town with such an intricate knot that an oracle declared that anyone who could untie it would be the master of Asia. Alexander, just twenty-two years old, commanding an expeditionary force of only about thirty thousand Macedonian veterans, knew that he would need every advantage he could possibly get to be victorious over Persia's countless host fighting in its own desert wastes. On his way to Gordium, then a Persian satrapy, he had already defeated a larger Persian army on its chosen battlefield beside the Granicus River.

It had been a fierce engagement. It broke all tactical rules. Near the end of the day, when the tired Macedonians had almost finished a long march, Alexander, against the advice of his generals, decided to fight his way across the steep-banked river and immediately engage the Persians who had challenged him. This he did astride his favorite horse, the white plume on his helmet flying in the van of ferocious fighting. When he gained a tenable position on high ground, he routed them. So when Alexander marched triumphantly into Gordium the next day and impatiently cut the Gordian Knot with his sword, he set loose a whirlwind of fearsome rumors about his invincibility. Psychological warfare had probably been used from time immemorial, of course, but this may have been the first known instance when it was used so effectively. Soon Persia's King of Kings was twice to flee the battlefield before Alexander.

Although the kingdom of Phrygia had expired, its mystique lived on. And so did its talented people. Phrygians continued to be the professional musicians in Athens for a long time. And as slaves, they were the most prized of all. Aesop, for instance, a Phrygian slave of Xanthus, a minor Ionian philosopher on Samos, was widely acclaimed for his fables, and still is.

Aesop had a brilliant mind, spoke many languages, and was sometimes used by the Samian government for diplomatic missions. He performed them with distinction. Aesop is best remembered, however, for his amusing fables. Many of them concerned dumb animals. Indeed, he brought them into the human family, and for sound reasons. They are also endowed with intelligence and feelings. For instance, anyone who has not been awakened at dawn by the prolonged hee-hawing of a Samian jackass, tethered on a barren hillside with scant weeds to eat, has not heard the full, mournful, heartbreaking eloquence of woe.

Rhodopis, a fellow slave of Aesop, was perhaps also Phrygian. She was a bewitching beauty. She went to Naucratis, no doubt with her master's connivance, and became its most notorious courtesan. Sappho's brother, Charaxus, fell madly in love with her there and perhaps squandered his wealth on her. His improvidence may have particularly irked his sister. At that time, Naucratis was a raw frontier town, less than a century old. And because it was a joint trading colony of all Ionian city-states, established by treaty with Egypt in the Nile delta, it was the riparian gateway to the oldest and richest kingdom extant. It was the world's premier hotspot. Everybody out to make a quick drachma was attracted there, particularly entertainers and courtesans. And any love affair involving a well-known Ionian would be scandalous gossip everywhere, much to Sappho's mortification.

Paradoxically, Phrygia's saucy cap, which was as well known in Naucratis as elsewhere, became liberty's symbol. For centuries after Phrygia's demise it was worn by liberated Greek and Roman slaves. In the French Revolution, it adorned Marianna's head. In Paris, it was defiantly worn by aroused street people in the storming of the Bastille—the Ancien Régime's bastion of power that cast a long shadow of fear in that teeming city. Its downfall signaled a new era for France, and for the Western world.

Phrygia was a gentle land. Its rolling upland meadows were punctuated by shallow lakes where tall reeds grew. Shepherds fashioned the reeds into flutes and played them skillfully to while away lonely hours and to soothe their restive flocks. The gods heard this music and fell in love with it. Mount Ida became their favorite rendezvous. There, myth tells us, gods and mortals found happiness together.

Phrygia's beguiling tunes were called elegies, but they were gay. They were full of youth's innocence and eagerness for life, evoking love's first kiss and a blush. They traveled fast down the busy Hermus valley and jumped the narrow channel to Lesbos.

"As superior as a Lesbian singer over all others." That proud boast by Sappho was justified, legend says, because Lesbos was steeped in music. The handsome head of Orpheus, torn from his body by wild Thracian women, drifted ashore on Lesbos's north coast and was adoringly enshrined in Mytilene. There it may have inspired Terpander, who won the first music contest ever recorded in 657 B.C. He also added three strings to the lyre, giving it a total of seven strings, thus helping to make that instrument the local favorite. Then came Phrygia's musical invasion, and the flute gave the lyre stiff competition.

Lesbians were more imbued with poetry than Phrygians. It was their daily fare. Slaves recited popular epics while women worked their looms. And women regularly attended literary circles where they recited poems to each other. Poetry was history, wisdom, and life's hopes expressed in cadenced form, easy to memorize. And it was entertainment. How many people could recite the *Illiad* and other favorite epics and

40

odes by heart? An astonishing number, no doubt. Memory preserved folklore, which included all past history and tribal customs. The nine muses who presided over the arts, we should not forget, were the daughters of Mnemosyne (Memory).

On Lesbos, youth's gay elegies underwent change. The lyre gradually replaced the flute as the accompanying instrument; hence the elegies were called lyrics. And they were usually love songs, which were something crassly new. Traditionally, songs concerned only important folk events or community events. Maiden songs, marriage songs, drinking songs, marching songs, victory songs, funeral dirges, and sacred paeans had obvious social justification. Love songs had no community significance. They concerned only two people—lovesick people, who were slightly daffy. For them to voice their feelings openly was shameful. That's why public acceptance of love songs was revolutionary.

Society, at last, had reached a degree of secure maturity in which individual happiness could be of general concern. So love, timidly, emerged from its hiding place in the heart and showed itself publicly. Hearing love songs, people recognized their own joys and sorrows and responded enthusiastically. And these heart-touching lyrics completed the emotional stitching together of society that had begun with Homer's martial epics, giving it more cohesion, flexibility, and enriched depth.

The Olympic deities mirrored this social change. Each god and goddess had several aspects of personality. This reflects the complexity of human nature: different divine aspects come to the fore as society changes and even as an individual's mood changes. For instance, Aphrodite, goddess of love, worshiped by Sappho, was sometimes Aphrodite Urania, goddess of the heavens and pure love; sometimes

Aphrodite Pandemos, goddess of all the people and guardian of family life; and sometimes Aphrodite Porne, goddess of carnal love, whence comes the word *pornography*. In the last incarnation, however, Aphrodite played a positive role as a prostitute's heavenly advocate, lifting her above defilement and destitution and making her rites, on some occasions, considered sacred.

Aphrodite had a love affair with Ares, the god of war. This affair was fateful for mankind, for Eros was born. Called Cupid by the Romans, Eros was a chubby boy with wings, who always carried a bow and arrows, with which he gleefully worked erotic mischief. Victims of his arrows would fall madly in love with the first person encountered. Accidentally pricking himself with an arrow, Eros fell hopelessly in love with Psyche, a beautiful mortal princess.

Psyche is the Greek name for the human soul, spirit, or mind. As such, she spawned the words *psychology* and *psychiatry*, the professions that practice them, and other things that pertain to man's mysterious spiritual nature. Psyche's story, then, is allegorical.

Eros and Psyche were ecstatically happy together. Then tragedy struck. Psyche's sisters told her that her nightly caller, whom she had been forbidden to see, was a hideous monster. So one night she lit a candle to gaze upon him while he slept, and was overjoyed, because he was beautiful. Alas, a drop of hot wax fell on his face. Eros awoke. He instantly realized in horror that the divine pact that had made their union possible had been violated, dooming Psyche to Hades and himself to eternal loneliness and grief.

Finally, Zeus was prevailed upon to restore Psyche to life, so that she and Eros could be blissfully together forever. Thus a love story was put into the heavens that joyfully proclaimed that love and the human spirit are well mated and nothing should sever them.

Thus, too, love songs that arose from earth, blending the musical enchantments of Phrygia and Lesbos, with Sappho leading the way, were not without divine sanction. This was heartening to the daring songsters. All this came together in the rapidly changing time of the Greek Renaissance, a time of innovation, increasing the fullness of life, its zest, opening up more dimensions in which the human spirit could expand.

Sappho and Alcaeus had a rare friendship. They were often depicted on vases, so talk of romance between them was probably inevitable, but no shred of evidence supports it. Nor did professional jealousy mar their friendship. He complimented her in tender words: "Thou violet-crowned, pure, softly smiling Sappho."

Alcaeus was a macho man. His interests were war and politics. His brother, Antimenides, was a mercenary soldier in Babylonia and may have helped Nebuchadnezzar capture Jerusalem. And after Alcaeus and Sappho were exiled, he may have become a soldier of fortune himself. Some critics, particularly the Alexandrines, considered Alcaeus Ionia's best poet, and Horace, copying his stanza, charmed the Romans. In his poetry, Alcaeus evokes Mytilene's sophistication and maritime character by fondly alluding to ships, wharves, wine and banquets, and a girls' beauty contest:

Where Lesbian girls, judged by their loveliness
Pass by, trailing their robes,
And all around them rings
Wondrous sound of holy clamor
Loudly raised by women in ev'ry year.

The phrase "ship of state" was Alcaeus's apt invention,

and he declared that true greatness lies ". . . not in well-fashioned houses, nor in walls, canals, and dockyards, but in men who use well whatever nature sends them."

Like most Ionians, Alcaeus and Sappho were involved in politics. And because they were Ionia's outstanding poets, they were naturally chosen to be spokespersons for Mytilene's aristocratic party in its bitter contest with Pittacus. It was a crucial election. We know about it only because its protagonists were famous people, memorable for more than political reasons.

About two centuries later, Plato selected Pittacus as one of "the Seven Wise Men of Antiquity." That posthumous honor was granted only to men who had taken some part in public life, for not to have done so, in Plato's view, was to be less than a whole man.

Pittacus's political career began in this election. He was the democratic party's candidate to be tyrant of Mytilene. *Tyrant,* a word of Lydian origin, wasn't originally pejorative. It signified merely one-man rule, like that of a temporary king. Ionian city-states elected their tyrants, which underscores their basic democratic nature.

Mytilene was currently ruled by an oligarchy. An oligarchy, or rule by a few, was another device of governance employed when political problems got too intractable for democracy to handle. This three-man oligarchy was composed of aristocrats, and their party, although a minority, determined to keep it that way. The irreconcilable issues that separated the two parties are unknown, but they can be surmised.

The mercantile class was steadily on the rise, always getting politically stronger and more demanding. They were a feisty lot. Merchants, agents, shipowners—all those engaged in trade—were the prime beneficiaries of its heady wealth. They demanded more legal rights and social privileges. At first, although considered indispensable, this vociferous class was looked down upon as social inferiors, particularly by aristocrats, lords of traditional wealth. Gradually, however, people began to recognize that commerce was as vital to them as agriculture. And the mercantile class, politically wiser and more socially polished, joined forces with the landless flotsam and other economic underlings to form a strong coalition. This gave them considerable political clout.

Should social prestige automatically reward economic success? Is social privilege for sale? Should "boors" be socially acceptable? Or should society cling to its traditional values? Such points of contention, sharper then than now, were to plague Western society for millennia, and spill much blood. Duels were fought by aristocrats over fine points of etiquette. So perhaps we had better find out what these traditional values were.

They were aristocratic values, of course. Homer made that clear. He made it less clear, inadvertently, who was entitled to claim those values. Kings, princes, and other nobility were what Homer's stories were all about. The common people therein were little more than animated bric-a-brac. The strongest men ruled; that was a fact of life; strong men were entitled to all they could take and hold—that is, within the bounds the gods allowed. On the other hand, they must cooperate for the common good, such as to vindicate their honor in the Trojan War. That lofty motivation branded Homer a hopeless romantic and assured his undying popularity.

The practical Hesiod, on the other hand, who had much helpful advice for mankind, has always been accorded inferior status. This forces us to conclude that although men may have evolved from the earth's warming ooze, as scientists assert, they left earthliness behind them somewhere along the way and grasped for things of the spirit.

The aristocratic values embedded in Ionian folklore, and highlighted by Homer, were a long time evolving. The only thing that mattered to Ionian aristocrats, however, was that they, the descendants of the Mycenaean warrior class who had won the Trojan War, were manifestly the salt of Asia, superior to all others. This spurred them to live up to their noble inheritance.

The common Ionians, however, felt the same way. They also considered themselves heirs of the Mycenaean Greeks. They, too, wanted to participate fully in their enhanced position. Unfortunately, custom clearly delineated the division of the two classes, demanding property ownership in order to be an aristocrat. And although this class distinction was blurred by the rising mercantile class, the people knew that they had to abide by custom.

"Tumult arises when Justice is dragged away, and whenever Eaters of Bribes seize her and give dooms by crooked decisions." Thus Hesiod complained of laws that merely embodied customs, as all laws originally did. He advocated laws tailored to people presently alive and clearly made known to them. *Eumonia,* a political catchword of gigantic force, would do the rest. It simply meant that law was recognized as binding. Greeks realized that freedom was impossible without legal restraints. And because they valued freedom above everything else, laws were faithfully kept.

As a result, Ionian city-states had no police. They weren't needed. The only semblance of a police force was in the relatively few publicly owned slaves assigned to civic magistrates. They might be assembled in an emergency. Moreover, city-states had no standing army to quell domestic lawbreakers. The militia was their sole military force. This was composed of citizens who provided their own weapons and armor and, in the case of the aristocrats, who traditionally comprised the cavalry, supplied their own horses as well. The militia, however, could be called up to fight only external foes. Custom didn't sanction its use domestically. Volunteers among them might be solicited to put down a domestic uprising, and this extreme measure may have been contemplated by Pittacus in the unusual aftermath of Mytilene's hard-fought election. Then a breakdown of government threatened.

With slaves performing routine civic functions, no police force, a democratic army that was cost-free, and wars that might possibly pay for themselves in rich booty from sacked cities and captives sold into slavery, it is easy to understand how Ionians could build magnificent cities with more amenities per capita than most modern nations can afford.

Obviously, "eumonia" set the Greeks apart. No foreign monarch could exact from his people the absolute obedience that Ionians gave to their body of laws. Sappho could throw herself into a bitter political campaign with less fear for her personal safety than, say, an American counterpart was able to do about twenty-seven hundred years later.

"The farther backward you look," said Winston Churchill, "the farther forward you are likely to see." This particular election, occurring within two centuries of Homer's lifetime, is probably the earliest one we can pry into. To ponder its outcome meaningfully, though, we should know more about its electorate.

Who could vote in this particular election? That is uncertain. Originally citizenship was restricted to property-owning males over twenty-one years old. But after Homer's time, the erstwhile sturdy farming folk, aided and abetted by slavery, had become Lords of the Land. They were now aristocrats, heirs presumptive to the original warrior class from which Homer had drawn his heroes. Then Ionian city-states, forever seething with rising expectations, did two revolutionary things: first, they enfranchised poor city dwellers without land; second, they confronted the fundamental racial issue. What made a person either Greek or barbarian? They decreed that Greekness was solely a matter of culture. Blood didn't count. The whole mixed population was thereby put on an equal legal footing. This, most people felt, was justice. Now everyone had a sense of belonging. Much later, Athens passed a similar law.

Heracleitus, the crusty old Ephesian nobleman, expressed the aristocratic creed succinctly: "One good man is worth ten thousand ordinary mortals." Still, Heracleitus was a conscientious citizen of Ephesus. "The people must fight for a law as for a rampart," he declared. And he regularly cooperated with the democratic majority, but usually in vain. The vast majority of citizens were not as farsighted as he was. His repeated exhortations for Ephesus to lead the way in forming a mutual defense with all Ionian city-states, for instance, failed. (This was Ionia's greatest weakness and led to its ultimate downfall.) As a result, Heracleitus had a dim view of human nature. In his later years, he preferred solitude and found solace in the vigorous exercise of philosophy.

The word *idiot* is of Greek derivation and originally meant a person who took no part in public life. Aristocrats did much to cure their fellow citizens of that omission, and they deserve their due. They raised the tone of politics, gave it éclat, and made commoners seek participation therein as a badge of honor. Government was a public trust, aristocrats argued, best exercised by men who felt an obligation to rule and who possessed the innate qualities, financial means, and lifelong training to do so. That sweeping claim, at least to begin with, was backed up by a rigid code of conduct: a nobleman must never tell a lie; he must keep his word, never take advantage of another, be cheated in a deal rather than cheat by a single drachma. In war, he must withstand all hardships, face any danger, and never lose his composure. And at all times he must treat his underlings, whether commoners, servants, or slaves, with civility and justice.

The aristocratic ideal persisted through the centuries, showing up everywhere in the Western world, illuminating drabness with light. It brought forth some of history's most brilliant chapters. Chivalry flowered. Troubadours sang. The Crusades brought romance to the Middle Ages and also, alas, manifested its poverty, ignorance, and cruelty, as in the wanton despoilation of Constantinople, a stronghold of Eastern Christianity, by Christian Crusaders, and also by encouraging the disastrous Children's Crusade with few adults to succor and guide it.

Nevertheless, the aristocratic ideal survived the welter of the Middle Ages to help shape the emerging countries of modern Europe. Great Britain, more than any other nation, successfully nurtured that ideal. The House of Lords, for example, is composed solely of peers of the realm. And the king or queen annually confers knighthood on distinguished commoners to renew and reinvigorate the aristocracy.

Sappho relished her aristocratic standing. She was inordinately proud, for instance, when a younger brother was chosen to pour wine in the city hall during the wine festival, an honor reserved for the best families. And it is easy to envision her finding deep gratification in teaching bewildered girls, just blossoming into womanhood, how to deport themselves properly, walk with grace, coax music from a lyre and other instruments, calculate in numbers, and find wisdom and abiding enjoyment in poetry.

Sappho was a sincere person. Too much character functioned too well to be weakened by falsehood. She threw herself passionately into everything—political campaigns, composing poetry, running a school. And although she was exacting, demanding the best from each pupil, her heart and her actions could never be long separated, if at all. She might insist on meticulously observing the minutiae of protocol at the school's formal receptions, but she presided over them with charm, and tried to make everyone feel comfortably at home. When alone by herself, she probably had her best times and her worst. The contradictions of her nature couldn't avoid shattering struggles, leaving her limp, as love left her shaken and emotionally naked, with all her defenses down.

Ionian elections were often rhetorical brawls. People supported their candidate in a haze of euphoria and vented their spleen on the opposition. For a woman, a noncitizen who couldn't vote, to play a leading role in an election was ordinarily unthinkable. Sappho, however, was Mytilene's most famous person; her fame, indeed, sprang from all Ionia and reached beyond. She was the city's most precious asset. That's why she was a spokesperson for the aristocratic party.

For Alcaeus and Sappho to be on the same rostrum together was indeed a drawing card. And what a contrast! True to form, Alcaeus lambasted Pittacus with invectives, calling him a splayfooted dolt, a potbellied drunkard, a miserly skinflint, and, worst insult of all, a low-born political upstart. For Sappho's part, she probably recited the steadily rising standard of living that had occurred during the aristocratic party's long regime, putting more victuals on every table. Voters would surely recognize that a vote for the aristocratic party, she might have emphasized again and again, was a vote for the whole family, for the well-being of wife and children, a vote for domestic peace.

As a candidate, Pittacus had a serious handicap. He was physically deformed. He may have had only one clubfoot, but that's deformity enough. Greeks put a high value on beauty, both masculine and feminine, and Pittacus was slightly freakish. He was not entirely unknown, though, and his reputation was sound. A minor aristocrat himself, he had been an officer in the militia during Mytilene's brief war with Athens. And he had challenged the Athenian commander to single-handed combat, as was the custom among opposing champions. It had been a strange encounter. When they confronted each other on the field, Pittacus had quickly extracted a net from behind his shield and hurled it over his opponent, catching him like a fish, and slew him. That seems to have ended the war. Pittacus was something of a hero, for he had saved many lives.

If Pittacus was a political upstart, he was certainly resourceful. He had an inventive turn of mind and also, legend says, an engaging personality. Like everybody else, he was a child of the Renaissance, striving to make the most of his talents. Now, looking back on that crucial election, which was a historical watershed, we know that Alcaeus and Sappho were the last great Lesbian poets, ending the Renaissance's initial phase, its poetic phase. And Pittacus was one of the last Wise Men, who were tribal holdovers. Soon a new type of man was to appear in Ionia—the philosopher. They were to have decisive influence on the future.

II

How had Ionian civilization progressed so fast? Only three generations, or perhaps four, had elapsed since Homer had inspired his fellow Asiatic Greeks to superhuman creativity—much too short a time to produce a sophisticated society. Only one explanation is possible. Ionia was already far advanced culturally before the Renaissance began. Then it was transmuted by Homer's elixir into greatness.

Let's take another quick peek at pre-Renaissance Ionians. Stimulated by their culturally advanced neighbors from whom they learnt much, they nevertheless preserved and nurtured their own uniqueness. One thing that set them apart was play. "The Greeks were the first people in the world to play," wrote Edith Hamilton, the late professor of classics at Bryn Mawr College, "and they played on a grand scale. All over Greece there were games, all sorts of games; athletic contests of every description: races—horse-, boat-, foot-, torch-races; contests in music, where one side outsung the other; in dancing—on greased skins sometimes to display a nice skill of foot and balance of body; games where men leaped in and out of flying chariots; games so many one grows weary of the list of them. They were embodied in the statues familiar to all, the disc thrower, the charioteer, the wrestling boys, the dancing flute players. The great games—there were four that came at stated seasons—were so important, when one was held, a truce of God was proclaimed so that all Greece might come in safety without fear. There 'glorious-limbed youth'—the phase is Pindar's, the athlete's poet, strove for an honor so coveted as hardly anything else in Greece."

Only a people passionately in love with life could engage in such an array of sports and an equal array of artistic endeavors. Both are forms of exhilaration. When people's spirits are blithe with freedom, they don't walk; they run; or, in other words, they excel themselves. And this involved everyone, in one way or another, and not just the few with exceptional talent. Even graybeards danced with verve. And so artists depicted them.

This is not to say that Greeks were unacquainted with life's agonies and sorrows and its horrors. They were always singing of the evanescence of youth, of life's brevity, and they stubbornly confronted tragedy with mute endurance, inured to pain. On the other hand, they found joy in the ordinary things of life. "Dear to us always," said Homer, "is the banquet and the harp and the dance and changes of raiment and the warm bath and love and sleep."

And always Ionians had their beloved alter ego—the city-state, the big pulse of life, cradle of democracy—to comfort and motivate them. *Polis* was the Greek name for city-state; *demos* was the Greek name for people; together they gave us *politics* and *democracy,* and the two remain inseparable.

Because the state's vital affairs are openly discussed and decided in a democracy, that awkward form of government, with its contending factions, is usually the safest guide into the future, but not always. This was proved by Periclean Athens. It acquired and ruled an empire under the guise of a democratic league, subjecting it to tyrannical dictates, causing grave unrest both within and without its confines. The resulting suspicions and abrasive strains were the primary cause of the Peloponnesian War. Thucydides, the great Athenian historian of that fratricidal conflict, believing human nature would not change, uttered the prophesy: "That which hath been is that which shall be."

Political campaigns thrive on hoopla. Flatter the electorate and promise better times, which means a little more of everything for all people—that is, if they vote the right way. That was the political gospel of Mytilene's aristocratic party. Later, Christian leaders, such as Saint Paul, used the Greek word for gospel, which means "good news," to describe Christ's message.

We tend to forget that the future is made into the present moment of reality out of what we bring to it from the past. That is an endless, seamless process. Clean breaks with the past never occur, even in revolutions; everything overlaps, usually for centuries. And because change takes place imperceptibly, it is usually not recognized until it is well established. We must bear this in mind when we read what Aristotle wrote, more than two centuries after Sappho's time, in his third book of *The Politics*: "Tyranny is the rule of one man to the advantage of the ruler, oligarchy to the advantage of the rich, democracy to the advantage of the poor . . . whether the few or the many is accidental to oligarchy and democracy—the rich are few everywhere, the poor many . . . The real difference between democracy and oligarchy is poverty and wealth."

The foregoing was written in the aftermath of Athens's defeat in the Peloponnesian War, when the superb confidence that Ionia had passed on to Athens had been broken. Doubt and scepticism had infected men's minds, like a disease. Aristotle's pronouncement was wholly false when applied to the election under our review, for the germs of future social disease are buried deep and may not appear for a long while. Sappho, Alcaeus, and Pittacus could campaign with

55

buoyant optimism, fervently believing what they said was true. Each could promise a bright future according to his or her vision.

However, with so much change about to become manifest, we had better pry into the secular trends and seminal developments under way in this election. They were already, to various degrees, making themselves felt. And they were to change the world enormously. To survey them briefly will help us to realize that our Western civilization, when measured against the millions of years that man has been on earth, is very, very young.

At election time, Ionia was in the throes of education; learning was in the air; the pursuit of wisdom was in the public domain and fashionable. Sappho was its exemplar. Her finishing school for girls and others like it in Mytilene are the first schools of any kind that we've heard of in antiquity. And being girls' schools, they seem like social freaks, educational phenomena that appeared long before their time.

Actually, they probably evolved in an orderly way, step by step, out of a plentitude of other schools or Ionia's similar learning institutions. In any case, they were in the mainstream of social evolution. Later, in the heyday of Athenian greatness, Pericles proudly proclaimed that "Athens is the school of Hellas." And Plato wrote in his *Laws*: "If you ask what is good in general education, the answer is easy: education produces good men and good men act nobly."

At the same time those magisterial words were written, Athenian education, for all practical purposes, had miserably failed. Sparta's education, on the other hand, had succeeded. In Sparta, boys had rigorously been trained to develop their fighting skills and their physical endurance to the utmost and girls had undergone hard training to build strong bodies to breed better warriors. As a result, the twenty-seven-year-long

Peloponnesian War had been won by Sparta and Athens had gone down to abject defeat. Yet Athens, with its philosophers concerned with the promise of man's spirit, rose from defeat and continued to build the luminous culture that was to be the Western world's prime inheritance. Sparta, on the other hand, soon faded into oblivion. Wars can change history. So can education.

Even before Homer's time, Ionian city-states had compelling reasons to outdo Sparta in militarism. Instead, they chose to cultivate mutually beneficial relationships with potential foes as a strategy for survival. This pivoted on trade and involved talents that served human well-being—agronomy, animal husbandry, medicine, the arts, as well as shipbuilding, metallurgy, ceramics, etc. In other words, Ionians realized they had to know more about many useful things to serve their neighbors well in addition to serving themselves. That was the main root of their education.

It is wrong, though, to think of schools in our sense of the word. Children were taught at home. Aside from Sappho's school and its few siblings, classes of learners assembled more like guilds, clubs, or civic meetings, involving mostly adolescents, but also many adults. Festivals, indeed, took in the whole population and were the greatest learning institution of all.

The most famous school was probably that at Colophon. This aristocratic town between Ephesus and Smyrna was noted, above all else, for its outstanding cavalry regiment. In peacetime, its meeting place resembled a sporting club. There Ionia's dashing young blades could learn the latest tricks of horsemanship, how to use weapons effectively at full gallop, and how to acquire flint-hard endurance. Only the best newcomers were accepted into the regiment. Then they could swagger around the town when on the loose, like perfumed dandies.

The effeminate mannerisms one saw in town disgusted Xenophanes, its most famous philosopher. He continually riled against aping Lydian ways: dressing up with fancy lace cuffs and collars, wearing false curls, and drinking so much that one never saw the sun rise or set. Such degeneracy, he repeatedly warned, was the best preparation for defeat and slavery.

Colophon's cavalry regiment, however, always rose above its sinful splurges to save the day. Do or die was its motto. And because the regiment put an end to every war in which it participated, Ionians got into the habit of saying, when they wanted something finished, "Put a colophon to it."

This sobriquet stuck. Plato later characterized Colophon as a timeocracy—that is, a state whose stage of evolutionary development had made love of glory its ruling principle. But history contrived another resemblance. Because Colophon was close to Ephesus, which possibly became the Western world's first publishing center, bringing out Homer, Hesiod, Sappho, and other Ionian authors and also, in due time, first publishing the New Testament and the whole Bible, its name, colophon, came to signify the end of a book or, more particularly, the publisher's concluding remarks and his identifying mark. Thus *colophon* became part of the English language.

Ionia's most ubiquitous and effective schools were, no doubt, associated with festivals. Classes to qualify for festal contests or performances, either individually or as a member of a team, were always exciting. All the arts, athletics, and group performances in song and dance were covered, and once a pupil qualified, intensive training ensued. Children were trained from early years and progressed a step at a time. Hence many classes were almost constantly under way.

The great festivals began in spring. So in winter, when Boreas blew and the countryside was bleak, preparatory training was intensive. Then hard work, plenteous companionship, and nightly dreams of winning honor for one's native city made the winter months fly by.

Because art seeks to give permanence to the fleeting moment, preserving life's most precious jewels above and beyond the ravages of time, it is a challenging exercise of body and soul to anyone. The word *choral* derives from the Greek name for the site where singing and dancing took place, giving us the words *chorus* and *choreography*, which illustrates the intimacy of those two arts. Both were dear to the Greek heart and spoke a language not simply oral, but involving the whole body and all emotions, so that moods and passions beyond the reach of words could be expressed.

"Painting is silent poetry," said Simonides, "and poetry is painting that speaks." These, too, in their several forms, were subjects of festal competitions. The great Athenian playwrights, heirs to this tradition, presented their plays at the city's annual contest in the dramatic arts. Even in their ripe old age, when Aeschylus, Sophocles, and Euripides continued to be productive, they sought the gratification of winning the city's first prize for a play, rather than as a needless addition to their commercial success.

The theater, some people say, is the best educational institution we have ever had. Comedy holds a mirror up to ourselves, pointing out our social foibles and hypocrisies. Tragedy confronts us with the horrible consequences of our sins. And it is a catharsis, purging us of our base emotions, allowing us to start afresh. The theater was unique to Greece, but its place of origin therein is unknown.

59

Sculpture and architecture, also related arts, gave man, in a limited way, control of space. These were heady professions, and learning them involved a master-apprentice relationship. To solve architecture's problems, advanced students probably studied under itinerant teachers. Some of their best works may have been displayed at festivals as models. Only thus could the public's reaction to costly projects be first gauged, whether rejection, lukewarm acceptance, or enthusiastic approbation. And by playing the whole Aegean circuit of major festivals, the public critique would be considerable. The Colossus of Rhodes by Charles of Lindos, for example, may have made its debut as a model. At its completion, bestriding the harbor of Rhodes, it was adjudged one of the Seven Wonders of the Ancient World. Standing 105 feet high, so that ships could sail between its legs, the bronze Apollo took twelve years to build. A consummate fusion of a sculptor's artistry and an architect's engineering skill, it was a magnificent sight for fifty-six years, until toppled by the severe earthquake of 224 B.C.

Likewise, a new type of city may have first appeared as a model at festivals. Priene, the masterwork of Hippodamus of Miletus, the first city planner, was certainly costly because of its difficult location. Phocylides of Miletus later referred to it when he said: "A little city on a rock, with order, is better than chaos in Nineveh." Priene was adjudged antiquity's ideal place to live. Spanning a saddleback of mountain about twenty miles from Miletus, its cool air deliciously scented by pines, Priene peered down upon a world far below—a dusty flatland, beneficently obscured by distance. Behind it rose a sheer escarpment of rock like a giant shield, but otherwise its panoramic view was unimpeded. Shimmering horizons stretched to the distant sea, and cumulus clouds sailed the azure sky like stately ships bound for eternity. Down below, other clouds sometimes drifted, cloaking the landscape in a veil of modesty, as if it was not quite ready to be seen.

Priene's business section, made of milky marble, was framed by a dark green piney wood, and so were its civic, religious, and recreational facilities. They were all on different levels, connected either by broad staircases or by paths of gentle gradation. All amenities were close at hand, but often just around a corner, hidden by trees or an outcropping of rock. Individual homes also blended into nature, and although their plots were small, their privacy was guarded. "Early Mediterranean was the style," a bespectacled Turkish guide would tell his group of tourists in English. "Flat roofs were for outdoor living, but notice the irregular foundations [now only stone foundations remain]. Ionians abhorred too much regularity. They loved harmony, so each house was a little different, perhaps with a distinctive Alpine touch. Harmony is composed of diversity."

His small group of tourists walks on a short distance and stops. "Here is the house," the guide says, pointing to the foundation on a corner lot, "where Alexander the Great spent the night." That was when Alexander, on his hasty sweep down the coast at the outset of his Asian campaign, took a precious night off from his siege of Miletus—stubborn Miletus, which refused to be his civic vassal—just to sleep one night in Priene. It was still famous in Alexander's time, and its reputation for civic excellence persisted for another millennium.

Was Priene a bedroom community for wealthy Miletus? A mountain resort? A retirement community? Those classifications would have been resented by its citizens. Priene was a full-fledged city-state. It was proudly independent. Subservience of one city-state to another was unknown. That would upset Ionia's delicate balance of power, its authority within the civic family. So Priene gladly lived on the frontier of the future, responding to change as its safety and well-being required and responding correctly for about thirteen centuries. How? Its education never stopped. Its odeum, theater, assembly hall, and commercial and political agoras had lively discussions that helped Priene's citizens to find the right answers. An example of its vigorous intellectual life was Bias of Priene, one of Plato's "Seven Wise Men of Antiquity."

Athletics, or physical education, preoccupied youth. They were also a public passion. In winter, gymnasia were overflowing with young men trying to improve their physical skills, and the big athletic games—Olympic, Pythian, Ismalian, and their local qualifying contests—were the most popular festivals of all. Pythagoras, comparing life to the Olympic games, divided people into three classes: the seekers of knowledge like the spectators; the seekers of honor like the contestants; and the seekers of gain like the hucksters.

Greeks valued honor so highly that winners in Olympic games were invariably hometown heroes, entitled to free meals for life. And because men competed naked, to avoid the hindrance of garments, the beauty of their perfectly controlled bodies in action was a visual tonic. Bacchylides praised Automedes for the absolute command of his superb body:

> In the five events he shone
> As the brilliant moon of the mid-month night
> Makes the rays of the stars turn pale;
> So in the boundless concourse of the Greeks
> He showed his wonderful body,
> As he hurled the round quoit.

True to form, Xenophanes ridiculed the rewards and privileges lavished upon victorious athletes, declaring that they brought no real good to their cities. And Euripides, who also loved to point out the absurdities of society, echoed his sentiments. Nevertheless, the cult of the body, in which athletes were like high priests, continued its popularity. Pindar, one of Greece's famous poets, wrote odes to Olympic victors and was handsomely compensated by their proud families. Athletic prowess, it seems, was almost a mark of nobility.

Athletics and education seemed to go together as naturally as body and mind. Nobody, however, defined their exact relationship. Even today, the relationship continues to be a hotly debated subject. It is reasonable to assume, though, that inasmuch as athletics made festivals even more of a fixture in everybody's life, its contribution to intellectual pursuits was significant.

From religious rituals to trade shows, festivals covered all aspects of life. Mental challenge and stimulation was rarely lacking, particularly in major festivals with itinerant bards, who were master showmen, in charge. These professionals recited the *Iliad* and the *Odyssey* in serial form and orchestrated the whole festival to keep it running smoothly and on time. They recited the *Iliad,* say, for two hours in the morning and two hours in the afternoon, for sometimes three days on end. They dramatized their recitations. Each bard had a distinctive style—one reason why audiences could listen to their two favorite stories over and over. The world's longest-playing serials went on from generation to generation.

Itinerant merchants dominated some festivals; other festivals, such as local religious ones, had no commercial activity. Major festivals were like small worlds unto themselves and appealed to everyone. Women could attend them in groups, but not alone, unless escorted by a male relative or slave. That was the custom. A vase painter has left us a portrait of a girl and her escort, presumably a slave, on such a visit. Her gown reaches her feet, and she holds it up in her bejeweled hand to reveal golden anklets. A simple headband keeps her windblown hair in order, and an earring is showing. She walks gracefully, with diffident pride in her blossoming womanhood. Her slave, who walks behind her, carries a small object that may be a gift for the local deity. They both appear eager, as if entering a realm of wonders.

The itinerant bards operated their own trade school on Chios—that was their home when not on the road, their guild headquarters, and the school where sons and other apprentices were taught the trade. Above all, it was a communal cell of memory, preserving the West's oral tradition for posterity.

Homer founded the guild, legend says, because he was blind, unmarried, and without sons of his own. He had to take in apprentices to whom he could teach his stories and who could help him satisfy the demand for their recitation. As was customary, however, most bards brought their sons into the trade, which was a demanding one. In addition to knowing the operational quirks of each festival, and the peculiarities of their audiences, they had to know Homer's works by heart and much of Hesiod's, Sappho's, and other favorites' works in order to have an adequate repertoire. This was because the foregoing works were composed, not written. The Greeks had no written language at that time. The Ionian alphabet had yet to make its appearance, as we shall see later. So our enjoyment of the masterpieces of the oral tradition, preserved in contexts and forms believed to be remarkably accurate, is almost wholly due to the community of bards that lived and functioned on Chios. They decided all questions of orthodoxy, preserving the verisimilitude of the compositions until they could be put into writing.

Perhaps we should sadly note the downfall of female education from its high point in Sappho's Mytilene to its negative position in Athens. There women were admitted neither to Plato's Academy nor to Aristotle's Lyceum, nor, so far as we know, did the preceding "glorious fifth century B.C." have a school for them, despite Aspasia's influential position. It wasn't until Epicurus of Samos (341–270 B.C.) came to Athens, after a brief teaching career in Mytilene, and opened his Garden of Friendship that women were admitted into a grove of academe where philosophy was taught.

Epicurus's disciples regularly forgathered in his garden to raise vegetables and flowers, discuss philosophy, eat their daily meal, and enjoy congenial fellowship. Epicurus believed that friendship, enriched by both sexes, was philosophy's beginning and fulfillment. Like other Greek philosophers, he was completely unlike religious teachers in the East. Greek philosophy was practical, not mystical. It sought results here and now. Logic was its tool, man its master. (Pythagoras was the only Ionian philosopher who verged on the mystical, despite the precision of his mathematical mind.) Hard mental work was the price men had to pay for the rewards of science, or philosophy, as it was then called. So philosophical discussions in the Garden usually concerned practical problems of living. Philosophy's job, Epicurus believed, was to put a man's present life in order. That might also be his best passport into any life beyond the grave.

We should also note that Plato and Aristotle went into temporary eclipse. It was Epicurus and his contemporary Zeno of Citium (335–263 B.C.) who dominated people's thinking in the initial stages of the Roman Empire. Both humanized philosophy and made it simpler. Epicurus, from whom we get the word *epicurean,* was popularly believed to advocate a life devoted primarily to pleasure. That appealed immensely to many wealthy Romans.

Stoicism was the name given to Zeno's philosophy because he preached in Athens from a stoa, or covered walkway. He advocated the resolute cultivation of virtues. That was the moral armor a person needed to cope with life's stresses and disasters. That, too, appealed to many Romans, particularly officialdom. These stern and practical Romans shared a sense of the empire's responsibility, which was awesome, for it ruled the known world.

Stoicism had many illustrious spokesmen, including Cicero, the great lawyer, orator, and statesman; Epictetus, the Phyrgian slave freed by his Roman master to study philosophy, whose preaching inspired many weary or discouraged souls to live courageously; Seneca, Nero's philosophical tutor, who failed to curb all the emperor's worst excesses, but whose essay on charity, read by Shakespeare, became Portia's famous speech on the quality of mercy; and Marcus Aurelius (A.D. 121–180), the Roman emperor who, loathing militarism, nonetheless dutifully spent his reigning years in military camps defending the empire's frontiers against barbarian incursions and finding consolation in his lonely tent at night, writing his famous *Meditations* (on philosophy).

The education that began in Ionia had its ups and downs, like the mighty Roman Empire itself. It was almost extinguished in Europe's Dark Age and then slowly revived, by sputtering candlelight in lonely monasteries, to help make the world what it is today.

A second social trend under way in Sappho's lifetime was colonization. Rugged Ionia had little arable land, and since Greeks had been settling there for about five hundred years, all free land had long since gone. Overpopulation was an explosive problem.

Early on, Miletus founded more than sixty colonies on the fecund shores of Pontus Euxinus (Black Sea) and all along its approaches, beginning with the Dardanelles, where ancient Troy stood guard. And Miletus was better off than most

Ionian city-states. It had leagues of fertile farmland of its own. Its insatiable appetite for grain, then, can be explained only by constantly recurring demands by powerful neighbors. The strongest monarch, it seems, trembles when his food supply is low.

Miletus's colonies, and others like them, were not trading posts like Naucratis in Egypt. They were permanent agrarian settlements. And they stretched along the Mediterranean's north shore, its fertile shore, reaching from the Crimea in the Black Sea to the Pillars of Hercules, guarding the gateway to the Atlantic. Nice and Marseilles were Ionia's most memorable colonies. These offspring of Phocaea, Mytilene's across-channel neighbor close to Cyme, retained an Aegean character that set them apart from the rest of unruly Gaul. Marseilles and Nice were thus more amenable to Caesar's conquest and subsequent Roman rule. Likewise, Ionia's colonies in Spain created a patchwork of dissimilarities that, continued by others, have always bedeviled Spanish unity. Some of Rome's greatest Caesars, however, came from there—Tiberius, Trajan, and Hadrian.

Trouble loomed when Phoenicia colonized the Mediterranean's south shore, its African shore. This was a fatal bifurcation. Phoenicia was viewed suspiciously in the West, as it had been in Ionia. It was part of the mysterious East, not to be trusted. So when Carthage, its largest colony, across the Mediterranean from Rome, attained imperial stature and began to act the part, alarms sounded on the Tiber. "Carthage must be destroyed!" thundered Cato again and again in the Roman senate. In the Punic Wars that followed, Rome was besieged by Hannibal, the great Carthaginian general, for sixteen years; he had destroyed Rome's army in the brilliant battle of Cannae and then methodically devastated the countryside. But Rome, behind its stout walls, refused to capitulate.

Hannibal, finally discouraged, left to fight less obdurate foes. Rome slowly recovered and then wiped Carthage from the face of the earth.

Ionia's far-flung colonies had their greatest effect on Ionia itself. Ionians matured. Involved in the Mediterranean world's problems, they learned that more only sometimes means better. Ionia had long since outgrown parochialism. Now its cosmopolitan outlook developed a heartfelt dimension. Almost every family had kinfolk abroad, and these familial relationships made foreign affairs more meaningful and significant.

Surprisingly, immigration from Greece still continued. Ionia's lack of available land was well known, but young Greeks, fascinated by Sunrise Land, wanted to follow the legendary wake of their ancestors and went there as the first step to further emigration. What lively scenes Mytilene's waterfront must have presented! Happy arrivals of young hopefuls from Greece and tearful departures of local "second sons." And sometimes, no doubt, the two commingled and sought the same home and future together.

Evidence of Ionia's far-flung settlements abounds. In the Crimea, Scythian jewelry of such exquisite workmanship has been found that it could have been made, experts aver, only by Ionian colonial goldsmiths. And far up the Rhône valley in France a wine-mixing vessel of bronze, thirteen feet around and weighing 460 pounds, standing as tall as a man and decorated with Greek warriors and chariots in action, was unearthed near Vix. And in distant Cornwall, visitors to the museum in Penzance can see lovely red Samian vases dug up locally. How did they get there?

Penzance, the abode of Gilbert and Sullivan's fanciful pirates, may have been regularly visited by the ships of Polycrates, the greatest pirate of them all. Most likely, Ionian ships were sailing to Penzance before Polycrates became tyrant of Samos, drawn by its fabulous tin mines. Tin was indispensable in the Bronze Age, being an essential ingredient of bronze. Copper, bronze's major ingredient, was in plentiful supply in Anatolia and Cyprus (the name derives from copper), but commercial deposits of tin were found only in Spain and Cornwall. How much tin is mixed with copper to make bronze? Two ancient peoples jealously guarded that secret. One was the Hittites, the other the Celts. Visitors to Stonehenge in Cornwall marvel at the Celts' engineering skill, wondering how they could have possibly stacked such huge slabs of stone into a symmetrical structure and why. The Celts didn't exhibit the same skill elsewhere. By Polycrates' time, though, such mysteries were passé. Then the later Bronze Age was merging into the Iron Age, and making bronze was no longer a secret.

Polycrates, called the Lord of the Sea, was the first to be so honored. His particular dominion was the eastern Mediterranean, where it washed three continents. There trade routes converged, and its numerous coves were hangouts for pirates. Polycrates relentlessly tracked the pirates to their lairs, gave them no quarter, and eliminated them. Then he took over that lucrative occupation himself and became the most fearsome pirate of all.

His instrument of power was the trireme, a new type of warship. It could carry more warriors and had the speed to overtake other ships. On land, he had a solid base of power in contented Samians. The Green Island, as Samos is called, was agriculturally rich. It also had a lively trade—legitimate trade as well as the bounty of piracy. Polycrates had a dazzling court. Ionia's best poets, artists, philosophers, physicians, engineers, and artisans were invited to reside there and to enjoy a comfortable pension. Pythagoras, a native Samian, was the leading philosopher in residence. He eventually found the atmosphere oppressive, however, and left.

Polycrates kept his people content by giving them jobs. Anybody could come to Samos, it seems, and find work. Polycrates was a builder on a grand scale, but whether his grandiose projects were undertaken as public works, as some scholars contend, or simply because they were needed is unclear. Perhaps both. The one thing certain is that he was the first of his kind, a full-scale Renaissance prince. He built magnificently, lived luxuriantly, and supported the arts and scholarship as only a fabulously rich and genuine devotee could.

One of his biggest projects was the harbor at Pythagorian, named for the philosopher. This work entailed building a mole in the open roadstead, the remnant of which can still be seen underwater. Another project, also a first of its kind, was digging a tunnel through a mountain to bring in water to irrigate Phythagorian's fertile plain on the mountain's leeward side. The undertaking was begun on both sides of the mile-wide mountain and met in the middle with a discrepancy of barely a finger's width. A third great project was the temple of Hera. It was the most grandiose of all and was never completed.

Hera, legend says, was born on Samos. The wife of Zeus, heaven's queen, the guardian of family life on earth, she was entitled to the best temple Samians could conceive. And only Polycrates would undertake such a mind-boggling project. The so-called temple, in fact, turned out to be a monumental city of lustrous marble. Compact in size, it was visible far at sea, a beacon of beauty. The temple itself was its core. But now only foundations remain. The cluster of buildings can only be envisioned.

The visitor cannot help but feel some awe and speculate. Standing on a large expanse of marble flooring, surrounded by others of various size and shapes, and with big fragments of columns, pediments, and lovely friezes lying around, all wrapped up in an empty countryside, under an arching vault of vivid hues, one finds himself in an ancient research center into the mysteries of earth and sky.

Polycrates was an innovator. He had combed the whole Mediterranean area to bring men of science to his court, and the departure of Pythagoras, with his great mathematical mind, was a serious loss; ergo, what to do? Well, why not bring the best minds obtainable to Samos and put them together in congenial surroundings in order to concentrate on those traditional twins—astronomy and mathematics? That is what Pythagoras did. And Pythagoras also used music, with its scale of numbers and its seductive soothing of human nerves, to build a ladder to the stars. So one building could be an auditorium for music to coax the mind to far-off thought. Another could be devoted entirely to earth sciences, telling us why flowers respond to the sun as they do, what makes plants grow, etc. Such a research center, indeed, would help explain the later presence of Aristarchus (c. 310–320 B.C.), the native Samian who anticipated Copernicus with the theory that the sun was the center of our planetary system, asserting: "The fixed stars and the sun remain unmoved, and the earth revolves about the sun in the circumference of a circle, the sun lying in the middle of the orbit." About two thousand years later, Galileo got himself into serious trouble with the Catholic Church by endorsing the Copernican theory and barely escaped the fires of the Inquisition.

Polycrates' grandiose projects cost staggering sums of money. To pay for them, Samians were encouraged to engage in trade all over the known world, to be more productive, and they were taxed as much as prudence allowed. That wasn't enough, however. Polycrates' relentless piracy was

71

needed to keep the state solvent. When asked, on one occasion why he captured the ships of friends as well as of foes, he replied that friends were more grateful when their property was restored to them than if it hadn't been taken in the first place.

Polycrates was very worldly wise. Perhaps he had grown too sure of himself. He apparently believed his judgment of human nature was infallible. That can be a fatal flaw. For twenty years he had played the rough-and-tumble international power game. Without territorial ambitions of his own and without even establishing agricultural settlements abroad like most Ionian city-states, he had concentrated his energies on command of the seas. His sole ambition was to make his beloved Samos, with its pine-clad hills where deer and wild boar roamed (the hunter and his dog were a favorite subject of artists), the indisputable leader of Ionia in commerce, wealth, and culture. Hence the main thrust of his foreign policy was to keep Egypt, his main trading partner, out of Persia's rapacious hands.

Persia was on the march. It had already overrun most of the Near East, subjecting much of mainland Ionia to a mild hegemony. It repeatedly stabbed at Egypt and sharply resented Polycrates' aid to Pharaoh Amasis. Even more, it bristled at Polycrates' bottling up its ships in Phoenician ports, for any ship that tried to outrun Samian triremes invariably lost. For Darius, Persia's ambitious King of Kings, Polycrates was a thorn in the flesh.

Sardis was now Persia's capital in the West. The satrap there, representing the King of Kings, exercised the authority of ordinary monarchs. Recently, however, relations between the satrap and Polycrates had improved. They had exchanged cordial messages. And perhaps the satrap had mentioned a substantive matter that had been a bone of contention between them, opening it to negotiation. And their trusted envoys may have met and haggled endlessly over details. Then, perhaps, there had been a breakthrough favorable to Polycrates. We don't know. All we know is that Polycrates was invited to a conference on the mainland and that he accepted.

It is a short trip from Samos Town to the nearest port on the mainland. Samians knew exactly when to leave to catch a favorable wind; it would bring them to their destination in a few hours, with oar power used only for docking. In all probability, no impressive naval display marked Polycrates' departure, no sizable bodyguard accompanied him, and none of the usual fanfare of state celebrated his arrival on the mainland. Again, we don't know. History simply tells us that Polycrates was seized on the mainland, taken to the Mecale Peninsula, and there, within sight of Samos, the Lord of the Sea was crucified upside down. Samians crowded to their beach for days thereafter, legend says, to behold the grisly spectacle.

One of the most far-reaching, seminal developments under way in Sappho's lifetime was the alphabet. Its name derives from *alpha* and *beta,* its first two letters. Ionia's alphabet, perfecting that of Phoenicia, is the sire of all major alphabets of the Western world.

It was a people's achievement, long in the social incubator. The ancient Mycenaeans had a form of writing known as a syllabary, a set of characters that denote syllabic sounds rather than sounds of individual letters. Even this rudimentary achievement, however, was lost in the long Dark Age. Ionians initially had no script of any kind.

Mesopotamian peoples, starting with the Sumerians or before, had developed cuneiform writing; this was incised into wet clay with a stylus. Egyptians had hieroglyphics, a

73

script that graphically evolved from pictures into symbols. Both scripts, though, were primitive, awkward, and extremely limited.

Phoenicians invented the first true alphabet. It had twenty-two letters, each a sign for a distinctive sound, but only consonant sounds, not vowel sounds. Maybe that was because Phoenicians, unlike Ionians, had no popular musical traditions.

By adding four vowel sounds to the Phoenician alphabet, giving it a total of twenty-six letters, Ionians devised an alphabet that was simple, flexible, and complete. It could be used to express any human thought. It was virtually perfect. Nobody has been able to improve upon it.

Other Greek city-states also developed alphabets modeled on Phoenicia's, but they gradually adopted Ionia's alphabet instead, because it was plainly superior. Naturally, civic pride deterred the acceptance of a rival's alphabet. Athens didn't officially adopt Ionia's alphabet until 403 B.C., the year following its defeat in the Peloponnesian War. Then its pride was broken, and it had the humility to recognize another's superiority.

"Writing is merely recorded speech," a testy professor once said. "And its long, long history can be briefly stated: it started out as pictures and slowly evolved into symbols. Words are merely symbols of meaning. Think about it. Think about it hard. That's all for today. Class dismissed."

Alas, the advent of the alphabet caused much juvenile suffering. It revolutionized education. Grammar schools—schools that coped with the structures and problems of written speech—sprang up in Ionia. They spread to Greece, Rome, and so on throughout the Western world. Inattentive children could now be kept in school on warm spring afternoons to learn grammar: "(from the root of graphein, to write): the science treating of the classes of words, their inflections, and their syntactical relations and functions; also, the phenomena with which this science deals . . . the manner of speaking and writing . . . with reference to grammatical rules," and also wrestle with grammatical meaning: "The part of meaning that varies from one form of paradigm to another, 'plays, played, playing,' etc., etc." And all the while the teacher is yakety-yaketing and outside the window the sun is shining in a beautiful blue sky and an important ball game is coming up and the big hand of the clock on the wall doesn't move, doesn't move, doesn't move.

Now we are adults and have long since learned to apply ourselves to subjects initially distasteful to us. And also, perhaps as recompense, we have discovered the greatest romance, the romance of truth, and are still enthralled by its inexhaustible facets and depth.

The addition of four vowel sounds to the Phoenician alphabet was not easy. To select the particular sounds most in use throughout Ionia, and also those most complementary to consonant sounds and those most distinctive from other vowel sounds, and to limit the number to four was a long voyage into frustration. To reach an audio consensus, many ears attuned to different dialects had to hear, judge, and agree. Mytilene, home of lyric poetry, and Chios, home of the bards, were undoubtedly the main workshops. Without them, our alphabet may not have come into existence.

Writing became a new profession. Several generations were needed for a sizable number of people to learn how to read and write, and even then the majority depended on independent scribes to read and write for them. From the outset, scribes were quickly absorbed into city governments to record laws, contracts, deeds of property, tax receipts, bills of sale, etc., and also as amanuenses to high officials. Many scribes, whether slave or free, rose to the highest positions. And as the word *manuscript* implies, they were the backbone of the publishing industry.

With a mountainous backlog of popular poetry to put into print—the *Iliad,* the *Odyssey,* Sappho's lyrics (the latter filled ten volumes in Alexandria's library) and many others—a publishing industry was not long coming into being. Egypt had set an example. For about two thousand years, Egyptians had pressed papyrus fibers into paperlike material, covered the smooth sheets with hieroglyphics, rolled them into scrolls around sticks with decorative knobs at each end, and delivered them on order to pharaohs, head priests, and the richest families. Such was the Book of the Dead. This famous "book" was seventy-eight feet long, fifteen inches wide, and profusely illustrated. For convenience and preservation, scrolls were encased in clay cylinders and usually safeguarded in temples, the property of a powerful priesthood.

"Paper" was plentiful. Papyrus reeds grew ten feet tall all over the Nile delta, and papermaking was a profitable state monopoly. Naucratis was its center. Ionian entrepreneurs could readily import paper rolls and get into the publishing act. Scribes were the hang-up. Publishing was done by having a professional bard slowly recite the *Iliad,* say, while scribes wrote it down. Two hundred scribes could easily be accommodated at tables or lecterns in a suitable room. In the beginning, though, that was only a publisher's dream.

With scribes in short supply, the nascent publishing industry was too fragmented to satisfy an insatiable demand. Private libraries were the fashion with men of wealth, and rich bibliophiles kept their own scribes busy copying books of friends that they themselves did not possess, a practice that was repeated almost two millennia later in the Italian

Renaissance. And all this occurred before Ptolemy, Alexander's ardent philhellenic general, sent his agents combing the whole Aegean area to build up his library in Alexandria.

Ephesus may have been the world's first publishing center. It had superseded Miletus as Ionia's leading city-state. In addition to its cultural advantages, it had the best location to distribute the industry's bulky wares, both by land and sea. It was also close to Chios.

Chios had become the largest slave market of the eastern Mediterranean. This had possibly started as an accommodation to Polycrates. He needed a ready market to dispose of his captives, many of whom would make valuable slaves. Chios, his insular neighbor, was probably pressured to oblige. So scribes, the publishing industry's indispensable tools, could be bought there.

Ionia's major contribution to the art of publishing, however, was made by Pergamum. This hillside city-state, across the channel from Lesbos, had a royal dynasty (this was after Alexander's brilliant career had made kings popular again) that built up a collegiate library to rival Alexandria's. The competition between them was fierce. As a result, Ptolemy II prohibited the export of papyrus to Pergamum. Struggling to survive, Pergamum developed its namesake—parchment. This was made from the skins of goats and sheep. Vellum was made from the skin of young calves. Both were expensive. When times got hard, as they did in Europe during the Middle Ages, parchment was sometimes used over and over. Called palimpsests, the reused skins often had rare texts erased just to make room for local trivia. Parchment was more durable than papyrus. That was its main advantage.

Scrolls begat books, or something resembling a modern book. Sheets were gathered in quires and bound together between two covers. This codex, so called, was made of either parchment or papyrus and was more convenient to read than a cumbersome scroll. Not until the fourth century A.D., though, did it become a prevalent form. That was the century when Constantine made Christianity the Roman Empire's official religion.

Christianity, building into legend Constantine holding aloft the cross and proclaiming, "In this sign, conquer," was catapulted into imperial power as the empire's spiritual consort and began its ascendancy as the world's dominant religion. Alas, Constantine's reign also saw the world fractured into East and West, with its suspicions and abrasive mistrust.

Early on, Constantine called an ecumenical counsel in Nicaea, an Anatolian town not far from Ephesus. He was determined to prevent Christianity from being split into many sects, which would nullify its value as a unifying state religion. Theological differences had become acute and embittered, threatening schism. At the council, some 250 bishops from all over the empire managed to compose many sharp disputes and to forge the Nicene Creed. It defined orthodoxy briefly, clearly, and acceptably. It is still a mainstay of Christian liturgy.

Constantine also moved his capital to Byzantium, a Greek fishing village on the Golden Horn, an inlet to the Sea of Marmara, which is between the Dardanelles and the Bosporus. It was the world's hub. There continents meet. There a vital waterway east and west, sometimes only a half-mild wide, teems with rich commerce. Accessibility north and south by land is also easy. The village's name was changed to Constantinople, and it was built into a magnificent city, as befits the capital of civilization.

The Church of St. Sophia, for example, was an early paradigm. Conceived by Isidorus of Miletus, in part at least, it carried on Ionia's tradition of architectural splendors and engineering marvels. Its interior is one of the most beautiful of any building on earth, critics say, and its vast dome is held up, it seems, only by the prayers of the faithful. Nowadays, when Constantinople is called Istanbul, the prayers are Moslem, for St. Sophia has been converted into a mosque and gracefully framed by four minarets.

Let us now meet the Turks, who brought Islam to mountain-girt Anatolia. They were newcomers there, conquering it in the eleventh century, only about fifty years before the first Crusaders arrived on their way to the Holy Land. They had come from the east and had been converted to Islam during their stay for a generation or so in the Persian highlands. That was their first encampment since leaving their drought-stricken homeland in Eurasia's central steppes. They were skilled horsemen and warriors, very hardy, and tirelessly adept at swift hit-and-run fighting. They were also susceptible to the seductions of luxury, such as hot baths and the pleasures of the harem. Now the masters of Anatolia, always restless, they chafed at Constantinople's lofty defiance just across the Hellespont, silently proclaiming its invincible superiority.

The epochal shift of the Roman capital eastward, recognizing geographical realities, was vindicated by history. Rome soon fell to barbarian assaults; Constantinople outlasted it for more than eleven hundred years. Finally, in 1453, Christendom's keystone stronghold had its ramparts breached by Sultan Mahommed on a night of the crescent moon, putting that lunar emblem on the Turkish flag. And the interior slaughter raged for days.

It was a catastrophe. Europe trembled. The fearsome Turks, the strong sword arm of Islam, were soon besieging Vienna, encircling Europe like a scimitar from Spain to the Danube, blocking off its traditional trade routes to the East. Thus began the Atlantic Age, when Europe's eyes turned west.

Thirty-nine years after Constantinople fell, Columbus sailed from Genoa to find a westward route to the Indies and discovered America.

The eastward shift of the empire's capital had had its trade-offs. Increasing barbarian attacks on the empire from Briton to Mesopotamia strained Roman military resources, fouling up its priorities and chain of command. As a result, political discord between Rome and Constantinople exacerbated differences in languages and religious practices and eventually split the empire and split the church. Thenceforth, the Latin-speaking West devolved around Rome; the Greek-speaking East devolved around Constantinople. Two strong polar attractions now functioned instead of one. It bifurcated the world, and despite the USSR's collapse, the Eurasian world is still culturally bifurcated.

After Rome finally fell to barbarian assaults, the Holy Roman Catholic Church (its ecclesiastical organization was modeled on the Roman state, with pope resembling emperor, College of Cardinals the Senate, etc.) took over the state's temporal power to avert social chaos. It really had no choice. It was the only institution capable of doing so. Gradually, the church played a dominant role in the governance of the West. It was soon contending with the kings of emerging nations, such as France and England, for supreme political authority. Socially, the church had a pervasive presence from the cradle to the grave, officiating at the rites of baptism, marriage, and death. This power base kept all but the strongest feudal lords, as a rule, faithful to the pope, God's vicar on earth. Politically, intellectually, and socially, things kept plodding along until the Renaissance introduced Ionia's rationalism into Europe, giving its peoples a new élan and sense of direction.

In the East, the Greek Orthodox Church spawned the Russian Orthodox Church. Two proselytizing Greek monks,

Cyril and Methodius, devised the Cyrillic alphabet (named for one of them) for the backward Slavic peoples. This modified version of Ionia's alphabet captured Slavic sounds in print, and it is still used in Russia, Bulgaria, and Yugoslavia. As a result, Holy Mother Russia always turned to Constantinople for spiritual and cultural guidance. Constantinople was its Star of Bethlehem in an otherwise hostile world. The church's patriarch was God's voice on earth, and the radiant city was the bubbling font of worldly culture. Russians shared Constantinople's estrangement from the West, which reinforced their own dark suspicions of Europe.

The Russian Revolution of 1918 put an end to its orthodox church. Religion was deemed to be "the opiate of the masses." And because Russians had no part in Europe's Renaissance, its Reformation, nor possessed a philosophical tradition of their own, they had to wait until the revolution forced their withdrawal from World War I for the works of Karl Marx, a German doctor of philosophy, to be introduced to them by Lenin and other communist leaders. Then Marx's *Das Kapital* and his and Engels's *Communist Manifesto* became the Soviet gospel. These nineteenth-century works echoed Hegel's philosophy of history with its endless class struggle, which echoed Heracleitus's tension of opposites and its eternal flux.

The facts of geography, as humans perceive and utilize them, eventually relegated Ionia to a secondary position. After Constantine moved his capital to Constantinople, however, Ephesus remained the capital of the Roman Empire's richest province, its keystone province, the Province of Asia. Confusingly, though, that provincial name was gradually applied to the whole vast continent. To preserve Anatolia's separate identity, "Byzantine" scholars coined a new name for it—Asia Minor. They also dubbed the Roman Empire in the

East the Byzantine Empire solely as a matter of academic convenience. The people who lived there had never heard of it. They proudly called themselves Romans.

Constantine-the-Great, as he was finally called, dressed sumptuously, rarely appeared in public, allowed a few worthy officials to kiss his robe, always wrote in purple ink, and was titular head of the church. On one occasion, he gave the church fifty vellum Bibles in codex form. This was an extravagance far beyond the reach of ordinary Christians, who came from the empire's lower social strata. Hence papyrus continued to prevail in biblical writings.

The Bible was a best-seller from the start, legend says, as Homer's works were before it. The Epistles of Paul, written between A.D. 50 and 62, were the first Holy Writ. They made up the nucleus around which the rest of the New Testament, and eventually the Old Testament, was gathered. Next came the Four Gospels and the Acts of the Apostles. The twenty-one letters by various authors were the last to be written. Finally, about A.D. 150, long after those who had known Christ on earth had gone to their reward, a complete New Testament was published. It was originally written in Greek, the *lingua franca* bequeathed to the Near East by Alexander's conquests. *Christ* and *Jesus* and *gospel*, for instance, derive from Greek words.

Publishing the whole Bible, however, took much longer. The Old Testament was the hang-up. To begin with, the Christian church in Jerusalem had soon expired following the stoning to death of its leader, James, the brother of Christ, by religious Jews. Then the Jews revolted against Roman rule, and after four years of savage intermittent fighting, Jerusalem was totally destroyed by Titus in A.D. 70, and the Jews scattered in their diaspora.

82

In the social welter that followed, biblical texts were probably difficult to find. The Septuagint, though, was available in Alexandria. Those first five books of the Old Testament, called the Torah by the Jews, had been translated into Greek about 250 B.C. Ptolemy II had brought seventy Jewish scholars to Alexandria to work with Greek scholars on the translation. This was a boon to pure scholarship, and also to many Egyptian Jews who had forgotten Hebrew. The Septuagint, then, probably constituted the Old Testament in the first published Bible. That Bible is still used by the Greek Orthodox Church today.

It was not until Jerome, the Italian scholar, who had worked for years in Bethlehem to translate the Vulgate version of the Bible, that the Old Testament, such as we now have it, appeared. Written in Latin, the new *lingua franca* of the West, it came out just before Rome's fall shook the world and helped to turn people's attention to Christianity when all things human were falling apart.

Nowadays, Ephesus attracts tourists from all over the West because of its stellar role in Christianity. In truth, Ionia qualifies, to some degree at least, as our Holy Land. There Christianity was weaned from tribal Judaism, survived the fierce competition of other religions, such as Persia's Mithraism, long popular with Rome's legionnaires stationed in Asia, and took its first bold steps as a world religion, offering salvation to everyone.

And there, even before Jerusalem's destruction, many of Christ's followers congregated. John, the beloved disciple, obeying Christ's command to look after his mother, brought Mary with him to Ephesus, legend says. Her home there has long been a popular tourist mecca. And there John wrote his Gospel, the most Greek of all the Gospels, which began: "In the beginning was the Word, and the Word was with God, and the Word was God." And another John, called John of Ephesus, wrote the Apocalypse (Greek for "hidden"), the last book of the New Testament. He wrote it on Patmos, a barren isle about twelve miles from Ephesus, dedicating it to the Seven Churches of Asia. And Polycarp, Smyrna's venerable bishop, was burnt at the stake to become Christianity's first official martyr. And there Mary, Christ's earthly mother, began her heavenly ascent to be the Mother of God. She was propelled to that zenith by adoring worshipers. Although two ecumenical conferences held in Ephesus failed to sanction Mary's theological distinction, her overriding popularity kept her aloft. Finally, after centuries of comforting Ave Marias and of the Angelus ringing its solace at close of day, Pope Leo V canonized Mary in 1875.

Isn't that the same human process that created Greek mythology? And isn't it proper? Can't human participation in creation be part of God's purpose?

"I am the Alpha and the Omega, the beginning and the end, the first and the last." Thus spake our Lord of the Apocalypse, his words reaching us through Ionia's alphabet. To understand better this keystone land where Sappho sang, let us leave downtown Izmir (Smyrna) and walk up Mount Pegus, which dominates the range of hills that separates this fascinating bayside city from its hinterland. Mount Pegus, I believe, is Ionia's best vantage point. We derive our word *pagan* from it. Early Christians lived in cities with churches to attend, such as Smyrna, which was a bishop's see, whereas pagans were country folk without churches. Mount Pegas marked the local division between them.

On top of Pegus is a medieval fortress, and one can climb to its crenelated battlement while inhaling the delicious scent of a redolent pine grove in its central courtyard. From that high parapet, the panoramic view is magnificent. Far below, ships look like water bugs on the sun-dappled bay. Eastward beyond the bay, blurred by a brilliant haze, are the distant mountains where the Hittites reigned. In the gradually rising foothills was a queendom—perhaps history's only queendom—whose Amazons, legend says, founded Smyrna. They also fought for Troy, Homer tells us, and their valiant queen, Penthesileia, was slain by Achilles. The Amazons were sturdy farmer-warriors who amputated their right breasts to better draw a bow and throw a spear, and they got themselves bred to raise only female infants. Closer by, just thirty-five miles away, was Sardis, Lydia's capital. In Persia's great days, when Sardis was a satrapy, its famous post road to distant Susa was covered by Persian post riders, riding day and night in relay, to carry the King of Kings's mail in less than five days. Closer still, somewhere where the foothills meet the flatlands immediately across the bay, was the realm of King Tantalus.

King Tantalus founded the ill-starred House of Atreus and gave us the lighthearted word *tantalize,* although his life was rife with evil. There, in his royal palace, legend says, he gave a revolting banquet to the gods that brought their curse upon his house, which included Agamemnon and Menelaus among other famous progeny.

That dark myth, repeatedly culled by the Athenian playwrights, was the source of their best tragedies. Their powerful poetry, exposing sin and its consequences, purged society. It is still potent medicine. One play by either Aeschylus, Sophocles, or Euripides, at least, is revived every year in the West's major cities. And playgoers still ask: Will more of their wonderful plays be found? Perhaps. A comedy by Menander, the last great Athenian playwright, was discovered in 1959. Called *The Grouch,* it portrays a type we still have with us.

Westward from Pegus is Smyrna's rich hinterland, and Ionia's heartland—the Ionia of academe. Twelve city-states originally comprised Ionia proper, plus Didyma, its religious center. Then Smyrna was added, making thirteen. Poor Smyrna! It was the farthest east, the most exposed, the most devastated by war. But alone among its civic siblings it still vigorously survives. Now Turkey's third largest city, and its chief port for exports, it's the usual stopping place for visitors to Ephesus, antiquity's best restored city. Izmir, as Smyrna is presently called (only Greeks now call it Smyrna), is the best base for exploring the forlorn sites of Ionia's other city-states on the mainland, which someday may be excavated and decently restored.

Squinting westward from Pegus into the afternoon sun isn't easy. One's vision gets lost in the brilliant haze. In the fertile valley immediately below, Izmir's urban sprawl is beginning to encroach on farms, spoiling a rural landscape that is otherwise harmonious. Tall, slim cypress trees, interspersed by oleander and hibiscus bushes, primly line the roads, and minarets point upward in scattered villages. Dust clouds are raised by trucks carrying bales of cotton or tobacco either to gins or warehouses, and also by women with kerchiefs on their hair and wearing red pantaloons, driving donkeys loaded with firewood. The drifting dust, though, is not all bad. It settles on dark green orange groves, light green lemon groves, peach and apricot orchards, or truck farms to make the soil more fertile.

One's gaze, though, seeking to resurrect Ionia's heyday, is frustrated both by distance and haze. Even so, each city-state's location is fixed in memory. Far westward are offshore Samos and Chios. Lesbos is to the north, Patmos, Kos, and Rhodes to the south, along with Miletus and Halicarnassus on the mainland. Straight ahead loom the spectral ruins of Ephesus, eloquent in their silent majesty, contemptuous of death. Closer by, Colophon's sparse ruins litter a lonely field.

One's vision stops there, for dear old Mimnermus is singing. He is singing a love song in a shady wine garden with his flute girl, Nanno, for whom he has an unrequited passion. Listen! D'ya hear it? A far-off wavering sound. Unspeakably lovely, unspeakably sad. Are those the vagrant notes of a love song lost in space, lost in time? Are they trying to find their way back home?

Reveries come easy. After all, this is the principal workshop of language, the stuff of lyrics and dreams. Here poetry took wing. Here Greek mythology was fabricated. And here, somewhere here, one of the most momentous events in history took place. No one heralded it; no one commemorates it. And because recorded history relates only a brief snatch of the human story, leaving it mostly locked in folklore, the principal transfer of the oral tradition to the written word is an occasion worthy of serious thought and worthy of reverence.

Fortunately, the cream of that folklore—Homer, Hesiod, Sappho, et al.—was captured in written words and was soon joined by the philosophers and the Bible to give Western society a solid foundation in spiritual form, which is the only kind that endures. Not until Gutenberg invented the printing press in 1546, however, making books relatively cheap, did Ionia's alphabet come into its functional maturity.

Rationalism and Christianity! Those two pillars of Western society have never had an easy time together. But they have sustained society by the tension between them, as Heracleitus hypothesized. They affect everyone of course, whether atheist, Jew, or Moslem. Society's infrastructure is their handiwork, such as making Sunday a Sabbath and, with rationalism in charge, constructing a constitution and body of laws for every Western land.

The Reformation, spawned by the Renaissance's enlightenment, was the major clash between rationalism and Christianity. And here, oddly enough, Holy Writ assumed new importance. During the long ascendancy of the church, the Bible had been subordinated to an elaborate liturgy and priests interpreted it to curious parishioners, most of whom were unable to read, to assure orthodoxy. But after rebellious monks and priests broke away from the church, demanding a simplified religion and an end to ecclesiastical abuses, such as indulgences, whereby sins are forgiven in exchange for a handsome donation to the pope in Rome, the Bible came to the fore as God's words, uncorrupted by man.

Moreover, Christians have the right, Protestants asserted, to learn God's will directly from the Bible. Indeed, the church's liturgy, conducted in Latin, had become meaningless to many parishioners. Luther translated the Bible into German, giving his native speech precision, vigor, and a new importance. The Bible was also translated into other national tongues. Now God could speak directly to his children, liberating them from spiritual ignorance. And biblical scholars worried.

How accurate is the Bible? Scholars shared the belief that the spoken word is prone to error, and the Bible unavoidably is based on an oral tradition. That was the worry. The oldest biblical text extant was the Codex Sinaticus. It dated from the fourth century. That left a big gap. Then came the discoveries of the Chester Betty Papyri, the Bodmer Papyri, and the Rylands Papyrus. These edged Holy Writ closer to A.D. 150, the approximate date of the New Testament's publication. Hopefully, biblical scholars sought a continuity of Holy Writ starting with Christ's disciples. And that, for all practical purposes, seemed to rest on the good fortune of papyrologists.

The search for Greek memorabilia in Egypt then, particularly biblical texts, took on a Christian fervor. Even so, papyrologists are a choice breed: brainy scholars, inexhaustible zealots, and academic nomads rolled into one. They're also very human. They'd rather find a fragment of Sappho's poetry, or another gem of beauty than countless nuggets of wisdom.

Another seminal development under way in Ionia during Sappho's lifetime was coinage. Like the alphabet and colonization, coinage affected Sappho and her coevals in many ways, even in its rudimentary stages. "Lydians made the first coins," Herodotus said, looking backward from the fifth century B.C. Later Saint Paul said: "The love of money is the root of all evil," but he was speaking metaphorically, for the development of money, as coinage is usually called, was a tremendous boon to humankind.

Human intelligence works slowly and also in brilliant flashes. Slowness and flashes—that's the story of the handy discs of metal used as media of exchange. Evolving from centuries of trade and barter, they also were an apt invention. The earliest coins were made of electrum, a natural alloy of gold and silver found in Anatolia's stream beds. They were made by Lydia's kings, probably to build up military prowess by acquiring more mercenaries, new weapons, or both. And possibly they were helped in the new technology of minting by Ionian artisans working in Sardis's jewelry trade, for the neighboring Ionians and Lydians regularly commingled. In any case, the marketplace, where the fate of all coins is decided, eventually asserted its authority, restricting coinage to gold, silver, copper, and bronze. These metals were readily available, workable, easy to identify, and possessed traditional values.

What made coinage successful, though, was not the intrinsic value of its metal, nor the easy portability and handiness of small metal discs. Neither was it the official seal thereon by the issuing authority, certifying the weight and fineness of the coin's precious metal—that is, the proportional weight of its gold, for instance, to the total alloy, expressed in karats. Rather, it was public confidence in the issuing authority's rectitude.

A coin certifier's credibility, in short, was indispensable to the coins' acceptance. By an irony of fate, that laurel of public confidence was first bestowed on Lydia's Mermnad dynasty, which, founded by Gyges, vastly increased Lydia's domain and wealth by betraying its Phrygian neighbor.

Herodotus relates that Gyges, when he was an officer of King Candaules, was compelled by the king, who was inordinately proud of his wife's beauty, to see his wife naked. Discovering this, the queen felt dishonored and gave Gyges the choice of either killing her husband or facing death himself. Gyges made his choice, took the widowed queen to be his wife, and sired a famous dynasty.

Gyges may have minted the first crude coins. And his dynasty rose steadily in military power and wealth for a century and a half, commanding widespread attention and respect. Its official seal on coins was readily accepted, whereas those of lesser-known sovereignties were not. In monetary certifications, Lydia's kings acquiesced to the honesty demanded by the marketplace.

"Character" was the Ionian name for a coin's official certification. Gradually that word was applied to humans, signifying a person's dominant characteristics—courage, prudence, irascibility, etc. Then it came to describe a person's total makeup. So when Heracleitus said: "Character is destiny," the word had already acquired its full meaning.

Man's use of metals, scholars say, most clearly marks his progress. After graduating from the Stone Age, humans gropingly, arduously, and slowly worked their way through the Bronze Age into the present Iron Age. We still live in the Iron Age, mostly because no other really important metal has come along. And *Atomic Age* and other maverick terms are academically unacceptable. Of course, all peoples have had a Golden Age, a long-ago time when rosy dreams were, in human fancy, actualities. It was golden because gold is beautiful and replete with other virtues: it's the best store of value, easily workable into jewelry and other lovely things, and the most durable metal, being rustproof and beyond all tarnishment and decay. "The apple tree, the singing, and the gold." To early Greeks, that was happiness.

Although gold was money's anchor, it was usually kept in the background, and values were computed in more familiar things. In Homer, oxen were the standard of value, and ox heads regularly appeared on early coins. Oxen were rarely exchanged by buyers and sellers, however. Rather, their values were calculated in swords, spears, armor, etc., or in domestic items, such as spits, pots, cups, knives, and spoons. The drachma, which is still Greece's basic coin, was originally the weight used to calculate the value of small quantities of gold used in barter, such as finger rings, long used by Egyptian women in shopping.

Coinage had its immediate antecedents in foreign trade, and this started before Ionia existed. Ingots of bronze and iron and bullion of precious metals superseded the simple barter of cumbersome goods practiced by merchant traders. The 'bullion trade' is clearly documented by an extant treaty between an Egyptian pharaoh and a Hittite king graven on stones in both countries, each pledging, the one in cuneiform script, the other in hieroglyphics, regular payments in gold bullion for shipments of iron to begin immediately. Apparently, the pharaoh urgently needed iron. It made superior weapons. And in wartime, weapons can be more precious than gold. Anatolia's iron ore, in fact, was more important than its precious metals; it enabled Anatolia to lead the world into the dawning Iron Age.

Official seals were put on gold and silver bullion certifying their weight and purity and thus setting their value. However, this required weighing a heavy bar with each transaction, for each bar was worth a small fortune, and nobody would accept its authentication by a questionable regime. Unknown regimes, of course, were always questionable. In any case, bullion money was only marginally successful. And Ionian shippers and merchants were those who suffered most from the financial hang-up. Their dreams and favorite topic of conversation must have concerned some wondrous medium of exchange that everybody would accept.

The international prestige won by Lydia's Mermnad dynasty finally brought together all the factors needed for money's successful debut. By the time of King Alyattes, father of Croesus and contemporary of Sappho, coinage was probably well launched. Alyattes may have been Sappho's host and patron during her exile and legend says he gave her a generous pension.

In the long annals of Lydia and Ionia's love-hate relationship, the meeting of the elegant poetess and the ruthless king must have been a pregnant encounter. Sappho, we know, had tender feelings toward Lydia. One of her favorite pupils came from there. And Sappho was entranced by Lydian fashions, such as upturned slippers, ruffled chitons, matching wigs, artificial curls, inviting perfumes, jewelry, fancy litters, which were the local limousines and taxicabs, and other luxuries. Most of all, the great Alcman endeared Lydia to her. Alcman, an Ionian born and reared in Sardis, had pioneered Ionia's choral singing, and his prizewinning "Maiden Song" won trans-Aegean popularity. Sappho must have always longed to visit Lydia, and finally, under sorrowful circumstances, she was there.

For his part, Alyattes undoubtedly hoped to use Sappho

in his territorial ambitions against Ionia. He was planning to invade his unsuspecting neighbors—that is, the prosperous and proud city-states close by on the mainland. To this end, Mytilene's maritime prowess could be extremely helpful. Would Sappho, bitter in exile, betray her hometown or any other Ionian city-state, as Alcibiades was later to betray Athens and Queen Artemisia was to join with the Persians? That's very doubtful. Her passionate opposition to Pittacus when he was in office, although contrary to custom, was open. Falsehood and subversion were not parts of her nature, and her love for Mytilene, and the freedom that it and other Ionian city-states stood for, elevating her to the very social pinnacle, almost deifying her, was an unbreakable bond. So, like fencers coming to a draw, she and Alyattes gradually settled down to a mutually acceptable relationship that endured for ten years, such as Sappho decorating the right banquet tables, officiating at festivals, and otherwise giving Alyattes' regime an aura of cosmopolitanism and liberality that enhanced his prestige, and thus earning her luxuriant keep.

History was to record that Alyattes invaded Ionia, ruthlessly assaulting Smyrna, laying it waste, and penetrating to Miletus before being stopped. But Mytilene gave him no aid, and he was turned back, putting an end to his military ambitions. Actually, his only lasting historical renown comes from the fact that he was the father of "the richest man in the world," Croesus, under whom coinage came into full flower.

Ionians were the chief beneficiaries of coinage, and they seized upon it avidly. It was their thing. They were the chief sponsors of its steady development and widespread use. Every city-state minted coins of its own. Even private merchants got into the act. For instance, "I Am the Badge of Phanes" appeared on an early Ephesian coin. Civic discipline soon imposed monetary order, though, and the competition to make the most beautiful coins got seriously under way. With steady improvement in minting technology, coins became exquisite works of art. Mytilene's coins, often embossed with Sappho's softly smiling profile, were noted for their precision and delicacy.

In due course, this new type of art, an offspring of sculpture and closely related to the gem cutting practiced by lapidaries in the jewelry trade, spawned numismatics, the science treating of coins. Numismatics became a new and valuable tool of historians and the hobby of men of means, especially antiquarians.

Numismatics' principal usefulness to scholars is to corroborate historical data that is otherwise questionable. It also opens a window on the public psyche and the economy's health at particular periods and provides portraits, sometimes exquisite portraits, of people and things otherwise unknown. Ephesian coins, for instance, represent many aspects of its famous Temple of Artemis, particularly its wondrous statuary, showing, among other things, Zeus bringing life-giving rain and the river god Cayster valiantly trying to cope with downpours. All Ionian coins, in fact, portray the full range of gods and goddesses in Greek mythology, whereas Lydian coins are monopolized by images of Mermnad royalty. That bespeaks a profound difference between the two peoples.

Numismatics was a late-blooming science. The first known collector of coins was Petrarch, the Italian poet who, along with Boccaccio and Dante, was a front-runner in Europe's Renaissance. He collected Roman and Greek coins in the same obsessive spirit that he copied classical manuscripts when he could find them, seeking illumination from the civilized glory of ancient times. Although he may have never seen Ionian coins, he would have been delighted with Smyrna's silver and common bronze coins representing the seated figure of Homer, and with Kosian coins with Hippocrates' head and the staff of Aesculapius on its reverse side, and also with Samian coins featuring Pythagoras, seated or standing, touching a globe with a wand. So, the coin said, the world is round, a debatable point in Petrarch's time, and dangerously debatable.

Several coins of Mytilene, issued in early Roman times (Greek city-states were allowed to issue coins of their own if they adhered to Roman standards, which made them readily interchangeable), may have come into Petrarch's hands, and they would have warmed his romantic heart. They commemorated Sappho and Pittacus, the once-bitter opponents, as long-ago civic benefactors who should not be forgotten. Ionia's system of values, crowned by nobility and faithfulness, must have impressed Petrarch very much.

Early on, the marketplace began to regulate coinage to conform to human preferences. Electrum, sometimes called white gold, lasted a long time, making coins of high value, but colorful gold eventually displaced it. Gold and silver coins became purer, and the baser alloys disappeared, giving rise to the adage: "Good money drives out bad." Silver coins were the mainstay of commerce. Gold coins were reserved for large transactions, such as buying real estate and settling accounts in foreign trade. Bronze coins were used by housewives in everyday shopping.

The long trend of improved artistic quality had one notable exception. One gold stater, a coin of exceptionally high value, had an original flaw. Subsequently, the flaw was corrected, but the public refused to accept it. Obligingly, the flaw was reinstated, and all was well. That bespeaks a very conservative public. In truth, it may have been a comparatively few rich men who were finicky about legitimate mintmarks on a store of value.

Beveled edges on coins were put there to prevent slicing away precious alloys. But no way was found to prevent governments in dire need of funds from replenishing their coffers by depreciating the currency. False certifications could do it easily, and Nero wasn't the only perpetrator of the fraud. The advent of paper money, coupled with the abrogation of the gold standard in the United States during the Great Depression, made this practice easier. With no gold reserve required to redeem the pretty paper, governments can print paper money galore, and do. The cruel nemesis is called inflation, but it's really monetary depreciation.

Money was a tremendous boon to commerce, so Ionians promoted it any way they could. Babylonians, Assyrians, and Egyptians had no coinage of their own until Ionians converted them. They taught them the technology of minting and helped them to devise a currency. This enlightened self-interest was rewarded, in a way, by the handsome profile of Alexander, Ionia's most radiant cultural son, appearing on more coins throughout the Near East than that of any other mortal or immortal. This was inevitable of course. Later Alexander set monetary standards to achieve a uniform currency throughout his huge empire. At the same time, he preserved local autonomy in minting coins. This turned out to be a workable system that the Romans wisely followed.

The world's first bank, legend says, was the Temple of Artemis at Ephesus. Only that prestigious institution probably had a sufficient aura of authority to regulate international currencies, which may have required setting rates of exchange, verification of official certifications, standardization of settlement procedures, etc. In addition, the temple pioneered such banking practices as bills of exchange, letters of credit, collection and payment of outstanding accounts, acceptance and safeguarding of deposits, and short-term lending to established regimes in urgent need of credit.

The invulnerability of a religious sanctum was indispensable to overrule powerful governments on sensitive issues. After all, religion and fiscal matters seem to go hand in hand; both are fiduciary—that is, both are based on trust. Our founding fathers subscribed to that solemn relationship; they invoked divine sanction on our currency, inscribing our coins: "In God We Trust."

The Temple of Artemis was never finished. It was huge, but its lovely proportions made it look ethereal, like beauty fabricated out of air. It had 128 Ionic columns, sixty-five feet high, with a slight bulge near the middle to please the eye with the illusion of symmetry. Each column cost a fortune, and their assembled grandeur was awesome. Here was majesty!

Here an ideal goddess dwelt that men could sincerely worship. Inside the temple, the statue of Artemis was the cynosure of tourists. But whose eye could halt at the physical goddess, no matter how serene, how beautiful? She was the symbol of a spiritual reality. In town, silver models of the statue enjoyed a brisk sale, which led the apostle Paul to denounce idolatry and thus provoke an uprising of irate silversmiths against him, forcing him to flee the city, as Luke recounted in the Acts of the Apostles.

The temple, though, which was large enough to keep its religious and financial affairs separate, enjoyed the quietude of sanctity. Visitors were respectful. Those who prayed devoutly were anointed with peace, so that earthly tensions drained away; the spirits were strengthened, and the right thoughts were brought forth to steer them. Alas, nature was not respectful. Earthquakes wrought ruination and were abetted by man. Now only shards can occasionally be found on the temple's forlorn site, for the lustrous marble has long since been carted away to be incorporated in other structures.

There is an untold story, a big story, in the temple's never having been finished, like Apollo's Temple at Didyma, and Hera's Temple on Samos. The story is simply this: Ionians, a supremely gifted and inspired people, achieved a beauty of expression in marble that no other people has rivaled before or since. But despite the dreams and painstaking labor of many generations, they were unable to fulfill their vision. It was a religious vision, of course, of things unseen, forever elusive. In reality, though, it was just a vision of what was best in themselves. How could it have been otherwise? The pathways to God are difficult to find and require faith to keep trying, and the Ionians never stopped trying.

III

In Mytilene, Sappho and Alcaeus and Pittacus had little time for religious concerns. They were up to their ears in a bitter election. At times, the campaign rhetoric was grand, all about who would guide the beloved ship of state into the unknown future. What did the future hold? Things were stirring in society, new and untried things, the full import of which, for either good or ill, nobody could foretell. One can almost hear Alcaeus thunder about the folly of changing pilots with nothing but uncharted shoals ahead. And Sappho could repeatedly point out, with slow deliberation topped with fervor, how Mytilene's sophisticated preeminence in the world resulted from, and also contributed to, unrivaled prosperity—a prosperity not to be ruined by allowing inexperienced men, untrained men, and unqualified men to mess things up! Well, even if Alcaeus and Sappho didn't say anything, they were still a regal eyeful. And how could such superior people possibly be wrong?

Poor Pittacus! He was such a comic figure. But he turned out to be a crowd pleaser, and people listened. Maybe he just pointed out a few cases of glaring injustice everybody knew about and asked what about them? "They haven't been changed and won't be changed," he would have asserted, "as long as the misguided aristocrats are in power. Do aristocrats nowadays serve the people? Who can be so blind? Anybody can see that they serve themselves! They used to be the king's noblemen, his best warriors. That we know from Homer. Now the people are king! We, the people, are king! The time has come to assert our kingship! Then aristocrats may assume their proper role! And serve the people again! If we don't teach them a hard lesson, injustices will continue and include you, and you, and me. Any of us. All of us. On election day, each citizen must act like a king and help throw the rascals out."

Well, Pittacus may have said something like that in one of his speeches, only much better. Anyway, he was elected. It was a day of joy for the democrats and of gloom for the aristocrats. "They have set up the low-born Pittacus as tyrant over this gutless and godforsaken city," Alcaeus spat out in disgust, and took to drink.

The election's epilogue didn't go according to custom. Sappho and Alcaeus couldn't reconcile themselves to defeat. They kept up a strident barrage of criticism. Everything Pittacus did, it seems, was wrong. If the election had been a close one, as it probably was, Pittacus found it extremely difficult to rule. The behavior of Sappho and Alcaeus, indeed, bordered on arrogance. That was the worst sin, detested by the gods. To conduct themselves shamelessly in defiance of custom, mocking the tyrant as a country bumpkin unable to rule, was an open challenge. Pittacus had no alternative. He imposed the customary sentence, and it was harsh, for in popular opinion exile was worse than death.

To exile Ionia's two most popular poets was very dangerous politically. It could have led to Pittacus's overthrow. The shocking announcement must have caused consternation throughout the city and agony to those immediately concerned. Gradually, though, sober counsel prevailed. Public support swung to the time-honored custom and the new, spunky tyrant who intended to enforce it. And Alcaeus, whooping it up with the boys in a wine shop, and Sappho, perhaps alone in her school, were left to face their personal tragedies.

This may be the best time, it seems to me, to confront the issue of Sappho's homosexuality. In the uproar raised by her sentence of exile, why didn't her enemies, or some of the fanatical supporters of Pittacus, bring that charge against her to help justify the severe penalty? If they had, it surely would have stuck in the oral tradition. Moreover, what about Mytilene's aristocratic party? How could that conservative pillar of society choose her as a visible spokesperson if, as later alleged in Athenian farce, her school was a hotbed of lesbian practices? Surely some of their daughters attended the school. But not a single whisper was raised against her at a time when recrimination was almost invited. Hence, judging solely by overt evidence, we should dismiss the charge as false.

Yet Sappho's poetry leaves no doubt about her emotional involvement with girls. She is entranced by the fetching way they walk, their beauty, and longs for their love. She is crushed when a favorite leaves her school to get married, which was a normal happening. And although she may toss all night in despair, with only moonlight stealing into her lonely bed for companionship, she wishes her beloved one well and happiness in marriage. It was an emotion too intense to be pleasurable and may have been wholly confined to her poetry. There it could be sovereign in a boundless realm of fantasy, free of worldly dross.

About two centuries later, after Aristophanes had popularized comedy in Athens, Athenian playwrights began lampooning famous historical characters. They magnified whatever weakness or vice they allegedly possessed, and the result was burlesque, smutty but uproaringly laughable. Not until then was Sappho stigmatized in a way that her poetry, always touched by beauty, would never evoke.

Greeks were outspoken about sex. It was a phenomenon of nature, no more and no less. Homosexuality among men was socially acceptable. No children were produced, which meant no mouths to feed, so it was harmless. Furthermore, it was justified, its apologists claimed, because society had to protect young women until marriage. Also men were often isolated in military camps, and in sports they habitually competed naked, for garments were a hindrance. For this reason, women were originally barred as spectators at the Olympic games, although, inconsistently, men often wore nothing among women in daily life, as scenes from Greek vases attest. It remained for Ionia's philosophers to take sharp exception to the practice of homosexuality. They condemned it as unnatural and offensive to human sensibilities. "Do nothing base with others or alone," said Pythagoras. "And above all thyself in reverence hold."

Custom required women always to be clothed. Only in militaristic Sparta were girls allowed to drill and to compete naked in games, like boys. Fortunately, the custom of female attire was easily incorporated into the cult of the body and was a boon to art. Artists learned to handle female drapery with consummate skill, bringing life into each clinging, wind-blown fold, enhancing the body's contour, and suggesting loveliness when not revealed. How much female nudity was socially acceptable is best illustrated by the fate of Praxilites' statue of Aphrodite, the most famous sculpture of all.

On Kos, both before and after Hippocrates' time, the people were rich. They wove the thread of Anatolia's wild silkworms before Chinese silk was known in the West; they built ships and were mariners; their fertile island gave them wine, raisins, and delicious fruits and melons for export. Moreover, their mineral springs and radioactive mud enabled their magnificent Aesclepion to function like a hydrotherapeutic sanatorium. Its Temple of Hygeia presided over rows of pools containing hot and cold water from different springs. One terrace was a sports field for gymnastic training. Moreover, art was enlisted for mental therapy. One small shrine had reposeful paintings for contemplation, perhaps evoking a patient's native scenery to allay homesickness, and the centerpiece, by Apelles, Ionia's best painter, portrayed life triumphant in the newborn Aphrodite Anadromene, the lovely goddess rising full-grown from the sea, her rosy flesh flecked by foam.

The Aesclepion was about three miles out of town in the verdant hills. The people who lived in Kos, the capital city, may have been jealous of it. Anyway, they decided to beautify their city and commissioned Praxiteles to make a statue of Aphrodite. She was the goddess of fertility, dear to Kosians, for agriculture was their basic wealth.

A master sculptor, Praxiteles could infuse marble with the texture of flesh, and his voluptuous creation, languidly poised before taking a bath, was so lifelike it seemed to breathe. Pliny the Elder called it the greatest sculpture in the world, and many experts have since agreed. In Kosian eyes, though, it had a serious fault. It was totally nude. One hand drooped before the vulva as if it had just dropped the last garment before stepping into the bath, but it wasn't effective coverage.

The Kosians, particularly the women, finally decided that Aphrodite couldn't preside stark naked over their agora. They demanded that the city council get rid of it. The council was willing. In fact, a neighboring city was eager to buy it.

Kos is a porpoise-shaped island swimming into the mouth of Ceramic Bay. Halicarnassus, Herodotus's hometown, is on the north fork of the bay, and Cnidus occupies the tip of the long, pencil-thin peninsula on the south. Kos is in the middle, within sight of its civic neighbors.

Cnidus was the Monte Carlo of the ancient world. It had a double harbor, one on the bay for commercial ships and a seaside one for warships. A canal connected them. And because Cnidus was on the main north–south shipping lane to Naucratis, its maritime business was steady and substantial. That wasn't enough, though, to make up for the city's lack of a productive hinterland. Just the city and its harbors comprised the city-state. That was all. Then how is it possible, one might ask, for Cnidus, a solitary civic gem, to be so brilliant, scintillating like a diamond on a stickpin? "Ah, dear friend, please step this way and let me show you," a Cnidian barker of the time may have announced, with a sweeping gesture of welcome. "You are familiar, I hope, with games of chance. Dice are more than child's playthings, as you must surely know. Here they may bring you a fortune. Just enter our lovely palace to find out if this is your lucky day. Roll 'em, and roll 'em high, and great riches may be yours before sunset. And you, sir, please step this way and bring the lady with you. Why not partake of the enjoyment inside? All noble folks are welcome."

Cnidus's location as a fancy resort was ideal. It couldn't have been better. Tourists were already flocking into the area, drawn by other nearby wonders: the Aesclepion on Kos; the Temple of Artemis at Ephesus; the awesome tomb of King Mausolus at Halicarnassus, which gave us the word *mausoleum* and which raised all eyes to the six-horse chariot on top, racing skyward like the galloping horses of dawn; last, but not least, the Colossus of Rhodes, where ships entered the best harbor of the Island of Roses by sailing between Apollo's legs.

Well, all that was stiff competition. In that big league, Cnidians probably felt that they needed an outstanding visual attraction of their own. Happily, they found it. They bought

Aphrodite from nearby Kos and planted her on an islet-throne of her own in their commercial harbor. Ferryboats slowly circled the islet while tourists crowded to one side of the ship to gawk, almost capsizing it, which may have added to the thrill of the excursion. On the dock, tourists were patiently waiting in line to see the most talked about work of modern art and simultaneously of course, with frivolity in control, to see what was ordinarily forbidden. Thus Cnidus's swank gaming tables had a lot of new customers. Later, legend says, Aphrodite was given a better vantage place ashore. Then her growing popularity promoted her again. She was housed in a beautiful temple of her own, as befits the goddess of love. Where is she now?

That question has been repeatedly asked down through the centuries. And history is mute. In the once-lively city, winds now whistle through broken archways and the rubble of masonry has been painstakingly searched again and again for Praxiteles' masterpiece, or some identifiable piece thereof, but all in vain.

Fortunately, the statue's early fame has preserved it for us. Artists from all over the Mediterranean world were drawn to Cnidus to see the statue and to make copies of it. The best of these copies ended up in museums and spawned more copies to fill our eyes with beauty.

Actually, Cnidus itself is a bigger mystery. Perhaps because gambling is concerned with numbers and the quick computation of numbers, Cnidus developed a clique of expert mathematicians. Here mathematics became abstract, enabling it to escape from its earthbound fetters of practicality, tied down by land measurements and engineering problems, as originally Egypt had imposed upon it. Greek mathematicians set it free to roam the universe and to be the invaluable tool of astronomers. That liberation, making mathematics the

105

language of science, was Greece's big contribution to it. Consider Eudoxus, a native Cnidian.

Euclid (c. 300 B.C.), author of *Elements of Geometry*, the most widely used textbook ever written, was a gifted organizer of geometrical knowledge, rather than a pioneer therein. This he acknowledged in a preface, citing the indispensable contributions to the text by Eudoxus, particularly his theory of proportions, which allows equal treatment for both rational and irrational quantities. Eudoxus used his mathematical thinking to map the stars, dividing the sky into degrees of latitude and longitude; and by better estimating the length of the solar year, he improved the calendar. Also, on the practical side, his map of the Mediterranean world helped not only local mariners, but all pilots who came into these busy waters. Altogether, his brilliant and encyclopedic mind produced seven books. If they hadn't disappeared as completely as Praxiteles' famous statue, one wonders if Eudoxus wouldn't be as well known today, and as widely acclaimed, as Plato and Aristotle.

Is history, then, merely a pointless record of fortuitous survival? Is the whole universe, like Cnidus, no more than a cosmic game of chance? Are all mortals, willy-nilly, just biological accidents? Is fickle fortune the actual master of all? Not a few eminent scientists think so.

On the other hand, aren't random happenings, momentary disarray, and occasional madness part of the divine scheme of things? Isn't the Dionysus thing, or occasional flights of irrationality, a universal safety valve? After all, Dionysus has been around for a long time. Perhaps he can be compared to a rebel God escaped from primordial chaos, an obstinate loner always on the prowl, refusing to settle down to a cooperative life and yet, despite himself, still a captive, caught in a fixed orbit ordained by the gravitational forces of larger bodies of matter, by the delicate balance of their divergent pulls, by "the mysterious mathematics of the Kingdom of Heaven."

Enough of such vagrant thoughts. Let us return to the orderly universe of cause and effect and bravely be finite minds trying to navigate in infinity. As a first step in gauging our rightful place in the physical cosmos, and in the spiritual reality beyond our senses, let us continue to learn, with all due modesty, about our cultural beginnings.

Symbolically, Sostratus may be our most illustrious ancestor. Another gifted son of Cnidus, he designed and engineered the world's first lighthouse: the Pharos of Alexandria, built by Ptolemy II. It soared four hundred feet, and although felled by an earthquake while still in its prime, it left progeny around the globe to warn mariners of dangerous reefs and shoals and to guide them safely into harbor.

Cnidus's greatest contribution, though, may have come from playing a quiet, secondary role, incongruous with its flashy character. Its school of medicine, possibly inspired by the nearby Aesclepion on Kos, was an important intermediary between the major medical schools at Alexandria and Pergamum, both offshoots of their collegiate libraries. As bitter rivals who claimed to be the indisputable medical leader, each was anxious to know what the other was doing, particularly with regard to innovations and discoveries. Cnidus obliged them. And it maintained good relations with each, despite its difficult role of go-between. In fulfilling that synergistic function Cnidus merely carried on a venerable tradition that had been the main source of Ionia's cultural enrichment.

Galen (c. A.D. 130–200) studied at Pergamum, taught there, and wrote prolifically on medical subjects. Pergamum's School of Gladiators, which flourished there in the early days of the Roman Empire, afforded ample opportunity to study wounds of all kinds, suturing of muscles, and human anatomy. Galen easily ranks second to Hippocrates as a pioneering medical authority. After those two Ionians, the world had to wait nearly fifteen hundred years for another significant medical advance. Then William Harvey (1578–1657), an Englishman studying at the University of Padua in Renaissance Italy, described the circulation of the blood and was hailed all over Europe for that discovery.

(Now we must note that Europe's Renaissance, like the Greek Renaissance before it, grew out of sovereign city-states, particularly Florence, Genoa, Venice, and Rome. Italy, as a country, didn't exist at that time. Modern universities likewise grew out of city-states. In fact, Europe's Renaissance was largely derivative of its predecessor. Alas, *the Greek Renaissance* is a bastard phrase, for that seminal phenomenon is not recognized by academe and remains officially nameless.)

And behind Cnidus's medical school, behind Sostratus and his pioneering lighthouse, behind Alexandria's famous library and its medical offshoot, and behind the pivotal shift of the world's cultural center from Athens to Alexandria stood the Ptolemies. No other dynasty has accomplished so much.

The Ptolemies had their summer home on Kos. There they enjoyed a salubrious climate while Alexandria sweltered. There Ptolemy II was born. And there several Berenices, Arsinoes, and Cleopatras—favorite given names for Ptolemy females—were born. They were a formidable lot, those royal females! Toward the end of the dynasty, they were stronger and more ambitious than the males, their brothers and husbands. By blood they were Macedonians; by culture they were proudly Greek. As Egyptian pharaohs and queens, or their royal siblings, they kept themselves apart from the native population and either ruled well or were unable to spoil the smooth functioning of the dynasty's established policies, routinely carried out by a venerable bureaucracy. Still, how was it possible for a foreign family to rule Egypt for about three hundred years?

The first Ptolemy, assuming the throne under the posthumous aura of Alexander's divinity, had that powerful spiritual force behind him. And he inaugurated compatible and workable policies that his two immediate successors faithfully helped to set solidly in place. They were the keystones of governance. And they adhered strictly to the Egyptian tradition, such as marrying within the royal family to prevent dilution of the divine blood. Moreover, the Ptolemies infused the ancient bureaucracy with new vigor and efficiency, built more irrigation canals, drained swamps to bring more land under cultivation, and worked ceaselessly at improving roads, harbors, and cities, particularly Alexandria, their royal capital. Above all, they gave Egypt the blessings of peace. Their military prestige, backed up by a strong, mobile mercenary army, kept would-be conquerors at a respectful distance. Egypt was a rich land. The Ptolemies made it richer. And their fervent and tireless promotion of Greek culture made Alexandria the light of the world.

When the sun went down on the Hellenistic Age, Alexandria witnessed the symbolic transfer of power from Greek to Roman hands in the funeral of the last Ptolemy. The freshly victorious Octavian, soon to wear the laurel as Augustus, had always considered Cleopatra a persistent troublemaker, who had nothing to offer but her personal charms, which were a far cry from her lofty ambition to be Caesar's wife and queen of the Roman Empire. So when word came to him that she had committed suicide, shortly after Mark Antony, Octavian's bitter enemy in the struggle for Roman power, had killed himself in another part of the city, he was pleased but wondered what he should do. After all, his uncle, Julius Caesar, had loved her. Mark Antony had loved her. And she was a

Ptolemy. So he decided that she deserved a state funeral, with the full panoply of Rome marching in the solemn cortege. Afterward, the two lovers would be entombed together, which, Octavian was told, was in accordance with their wishes. It was a fitting tribute to the last queen of Egypt, and its traditional formality was a promising start for the first Roman emperor, who, realizing he had much to learn from the tumultuous past, was resolved to learn it, for his future responsibilities, he knew, would be formidable.

Pittacus ruled Mytilene for ten years and then abdicated. He had ruled well. He was among the last of the beneficent tyrants. Later Plato and Aristotle rightly condemned such absolute authority as inherently corruptible and therefore the worst form of government. Pittacus continued to serve Mytilene after his abdication, and he and Sappho briefly shared a civic glory, as we shall see. His true historical worth, however, is manifold. He was more than one of the last Wise Men and a precursor of the philosophers. A child of the Renaissance, he was a prolific innovator; at the same time, he exemplified the folklore from which he derived his empirical wisdom. That folklore, which was the people's daily fare in Ionia, whether for inspiration, instruction, or entertainment, was almost inexhaustibly rich. It covered practically all human experience within the purview of Western man. For instance, it gave us, among other things, the four cardinal virtues that are supposed to help us most in the business of living. The virtues are: courage, temperance, wisdom, and justice.

Pythagoras may have been the first to voice this quartet of virtues, giving it distinction and greater currency. It was the product of countless generations of living, however, and came from folklore, not philosophy. Although the virtues have a synergetic relationship, Ionians accepted them on their individual merits and subconsciously absorbed them into their natures. They had been nurtured on them since childhood. Naturally, the virtues varied in each individual, from barely perceptible to considerable, but Pittacus plainly exemplified them all.

Pittacus displayed courage when he challenged the Athenian commander to personal combat, despite his own physical handicap. And it took courage to accept the democratic party's nomination to be tyrant, thereby inviting, as a minor aristocrat, the enmity of his whole class, whether he won or lost. And early in his regime he again displayed courage when he exiled Mytilene's, and indeed Ionia's, two most popular poets, putting his political survival at risk. Naturally, Pittacus had to use courage every day of his life, one way or another. And it had to be balanced with prudence, for raw courage can otherwise do foolish things.

There were numerous times, though, when Pittacus condemned himself for lack of courage. In order to assuage contentious political factions, for instance, he sometimes made concessions that he later regretted. Compromise is almost always necessary, he knew, but the degree thereof can be galling. Expedience! That is the key to everything, it seems. It is indispensable to politics of course, but it is also its bane. And because what is morally right, in his opinion, and what is politically feasible are often far apart, he had been forced to make many agonizing decisions. Also, he had soon learnt that to impose a law too far ahead of public opinion can have horrendous results. Tumult may ensue, setting society further back than where it was before.

The politician's job is to devise workable solutions to social problems; otherwise, they are not solutions. That's a sobering responsibility. And because workability depends upon the public's temper at the time, who can gauge it accurately? Here Pittacus had self-inflicted troubles. In his first term in office, he had moved resolutely ahead, disregarding minor complaints. Perhaps he had moved too far ahead. That had brought a reaction. As a result, he may have become too cautious. Anyway, his conscience bothered him. Had his estimates of political feasibility become too conservative? Was he subconsciously avoiding political fights? Was he losing his nerve? For injustice to prevail because he lacked moral grit and stamina was intolerable. Where was his old flaming faith? His zest? His resolution? If they were gone, was he fit to be a tyrant? Should he abdicate? After all, he was in his third term now. It was a vexing term. Hadn't he slept with worry long enough?

Pittacus thought it over, listened to the inward counsel of temperence, and decided to abdicate. Publicly, he simply confessed that he was tired and wanted to enjoy the good life. Before leaving office, though, he had to share power a little longer with Dion, his new deputy. Dion had to learn how to handle all troublesome matters until the next election. Then citizens would choose a new tyrant or, possibly, decide to return to the pure democracy of their recent forebears.

That decision lifted a tremendous weight from Pittacus's shoulders. Now, at long last, he could pardon Sappho and Alcaeus. They could return home. And everyone, he fondly hoped, would be happier.

The friends of Sappho and Alcaeus had pleaded with him for a pardon many times, citing the messages they had received from Mytilene's most illustrious son and daughter, confessing their desperate homesickness. The democratic regime, Pittacus knew, was now solidly entrenched. The two poets were no longer a menace, even if they wanted to be, which he doubted. Furthermore, he had cogent reasons for wanting them home. When asked why he had pardoned them, however, he merely said, "Forgiveness is better than vengeance."

That avowal by Pittacus was extremely radical. It was unheard of. Nobody had said it before. The popular morality of the time was brutally simple: do all the good things one possibly could for one's friends and inflict all possible harm on one's foes. That ancient moral formula, encrusted with revenge and hate, dank with blood, may have been publicly disavowed by Pittacus for the first time. It was a social shock. But then, unexpected things were expected of Pittacus, and the people were pleased.

Because of his responsibilities as tyrant, Pittacus had felt the loss of Sappho and Alcaeus from the outset. They had been the city's magic yeast; they had added sparkle to life, enhanced local pride, sharpened the competitive spirit. It was an intangible thing of course, but Pittacus, more than anyone else in Mytilene, had felt it keenly. Because of it, he had allocated more funds to festivals than he had wanted to, just to cheer people up. Indeed, the exile of Sappho and Alcaeus, although unavoidable, had been his regime's secret sore spot, creating, at least for him, an aching void. Now he looked forward to devoting much of his time, as a private citizen, to helping the poets regain their old prominence in civic affairs. That wouldn't be an easy task. Their families were adamantly unforgiving. They had been hostile to everything he had done, and his occasional attempts at reconciliation had been coldly rejected.

Nevertheless, Pittacus and Dion kept avidly working out provisional plans for Sappho and Alcaeus to be actively involved in civic affairs. Their rare talents were sorely needed. Of course they must be granted honoraria with elaborate ceremonies to bolster their sensitive egos, and to give them some

113

funds, which they might need very much. Alcaeus would be offered the post of military counselor with the rank of general, and he should be pleased. He would instruct Mytilene's militia on the new techniques of warfare that he had observed abroad, and mock military engagements would be arranged for practical instruction.

Sappho's civic post, and the one Pittacus and Dion fervently hoped she would accept, would be strictly honorary. But its importance couldn't be exaggerated. Fortunately, she was due home at just the right time. The spring festivals would soon begin. That's when final competitions would be held to select the best athletes and artists, both individuals and teams, to represent Mytilene in the forthcoming Olympic games, for this was a quadruple year.

Preparation for the games had looked rosy until recently. Then things had suddenly slumped, sort of fallen apart. Why? Nobody knew. Perhaps from overtraining. It had been a long grind for everyone. The dance and choral teams were the biggest worry. They had always been Mytilene's pride and joy. And this year's teams looked exceptionally promising. If they could win in the Olympics and bring back to Mytilene the two most coveted trophies, everybody would be ecstatic. And now both teams were in an awful rut. Their coaches were frantic. Something had to be done.

Discussing the matter, Pittacus and Dion couldn't sit still. They were too worked up. Leaving the city hall, they walked out into the agora, greeting old friends and always being respectfully acknowledged by passersby. They seemed to enjoy commingling with people, drawing strength from them. And they had a rare talent. They could focus on a problem and retain it clearly in mind while they talked with friends, asked questions, listened to answers, and cordially took leave of them. Then they promptly resumed their discussion as if it had never been interrupted. It was apparently an old habit.

Seeing the tyrant and his deputy walking together, absorbed in thought, people said something important was brewing—perhaps something good, perhaps bad. They would start guessing, and the gossip would spread.

Pittacus and Dion left the political agora and walked into the commercial agora. Here it was crowded, noisy, and hectic. They had to walk slowly. People were respectful, though, and deferentially made way for them. In the produce market, they enjoyed inspecting the colorful array of vegetables and talking with the women vendors, bright kerchiefs on their hair. The purple eggplant, yellow carrots, red and green peppers, cucumbers, string beans, and white melons were imports from Kos, Rhodes, and Cyprus. Local vegetables wouldn't come to market for three weeks or so. Pittacus and Dion sniffed and breathed deeply. The familiar odors were heartening. Farmers themselves, they were refreshed by the comforting sights and smells and the venerable complaints about crops, prices, and the fickle weather.

"When the women vendors are smiling, nothing is really bad," Pittacus said as they left the marketplace.

"All of them weren't smiling," Dion said matter-of-factly.

"Ah, but the prettiest one smiled," Pittacus replied. "That's a good omen."

They quickened their pace as they passed a noisy gymnasium. They weren't ready to get involved in the city's prefestival gloom. Likewise, they kept their distance from playing fields where sweaty youngsters were dutifully training and the coaches sometimes barking at them. They did pause in a quiet residential section, however, to admire the exquisite black-and-white pebble walkway being installed by a master craftsman and three apprentices, depicting dolphins disporting themselves at sea. They also chatted with a housewife and her female slave who were washing down a newly completed section of the mosaic walkway. They were making it immaculate, like the city's other walkways.

The two men crossed a rocky brow of a hill, inhaling deeply the bracing smell of basil. They descended to an isolated fishing cove, its quietude broken only by the occasional cry of seabirds. They talked to fishermen, who were even more taciturn than farmers, and heard about their diminishing catch; they watched them and their womenfolk sitting on the ground repairing fishing nets with swiftly moving hands or crouched on their heels beating octopi with staves, making them tender and succulent. Five small houses, boats drawn up on the strand, goats tethered on the hillside, children playing—it was a picture of contentment, framed by the boundless sea.

Pittacus and Dion circled back toward the city, lifting their eyes occasionally to the acropolis, its milky marble catching the first rosy gleams of the dying day. Shrines and temples to the gods were the first to greet each day and the last to watch it depart. They were heartening to look up to, reminding humans of their divine relationship and of their obligation to show it.

Back in the agora, Pittacus and Dion paused in front of City Hall to exchange a few words with a bearded sculptor and an apprentice working on a statue to Poseidon. They marveled at the masterful face emerging from the block of marble, mutely testifying to man's urge to create and his considerable ability to do so. Then they went inside.

Anxious amanuenses awaited them. They had urgent messages. Mytilene's preoccupied rulers were not ready to listen, though. Not yet. They had been gone less than two hours, and it had been well spent. They had found a cure for the city's psychic depression. The psyche, of course, is the only thing human that can be depressed. It is the body's

116

commander in chief. It can deprive a person of the ability to move a single muscle or of the desire to live at all.

Pittacus and Dion had considered all alternatives. And they always came back to Sappho. She could cure the afflicted contestants upon whom Mytilene had pinned its hopes better than anyone else. She, and probably she alone, could inspire the faith, enthusiasm, and self-confidence to make the final weeks of training, the crucial weeks, a preamble to victory. Her return was a godsend. And she was due home soon. If she would visit and address each training group to the limit of her time and strength, that might be the magic remedy, the psychic tonic to turn things around. And once she realized how badly Mytilene needed to win championships again, especially the two most coveted victories, she would throw herself wholeheartedly into the effort. Pittacus was convinced of that.

To begin with, Dion would appoint Sappho the honorary patroness of the festival of Aphrodite. That was the first major festival of spring. Its main events, extending over three exciting days, were the elimination contests in choral singing and the dance. Spectators were always thrilled by them. They were the most popular of the arts. And the grand finale, when the winning dance and choral teams performed together, always brought the festival to a hysterical climax. If those teams would bring back the prized trophies from the subsequent big Greek games, everybody would be walking on air.

Discussing the possibility of the public's elation after years of disappointment, Pittacus and Dion began overflowing with enthusiasm. With a civic triumph finally in view, how could their planning be moderate?

"How about Alcaeus?" Dion demanded. "He has tremendous appeal to young men. Surely he can help, too."

"Stop!" Pittacus finally interjected. "We'll discuss this later, Dion. Other duties may need our attention." He turned to the amanuenses. "Now it's your turn. Please follow the usual procedure. Give us the worst news first."

Like all Ionians, Pittacus and Dion were naturally ebullient. Going to extremes was easy. So temperance, calling a halt to excesses, was rudely intrusive. It was unwelcome, bothersome, a detested killjoy. Yet, in everyone's sober judgment, it was indispensable.

Pittacus had learned that lesson early in his regime. In the anxious days following the exile of Alcaeus and Sappho, he had had to face up to Mytilene's serious drinking problem. He had tried to ignore it, but it wouldn't go away. Something had to be done about it. So Pittacus, as tyrant, boldly decreed an ordinance that doubled the penalties for all violations of law committed under the influence of intoxicating drink. Surprisingly, no public outcry ensued. The law was well received. It worked. Excessive drinking in public places abated. And because that singular law has come down to us through antiquity's murky history, the message is clear: temperance was indeed a cardinal virtue.

"Nothing in excess." "Avoid extremes." "The Golden Mean is best." Such oracular axioms, seemingly as old as time, were born of social imperatives. Man's primitive nature, prone to violence, had to be quelled. Otherwise, tribal society could not exist. To that end, medicine men supplemented the authority of tribal chiefs, invoking the wrath of fearsome gods upon lawbreakers, condemning them to suffering after death. Thus *Homo sapiens* began his long psychiatric training, comparable to a geological age, in which he developed sociability. The process was known to the sibyls of Didyma and Delphi, who could peer deep into the past and understand all mysteries and then would explain them in riddles. Afterward, having passed through life's rude kindergarten, men had minds of their own and wanted to know many things.

"Wealth without virtue makes a bad neighbor." That remark by Sappho after her return from exile may have referred either to Lydia or, more likely, to a new and ostentatious neighbor. In any case, vulgar display of wealth was considered flagrant bad taste. Ionians were too conscious of the hard toil required to earn a living to condone waste of any kind. To Sappho, particularly after her suffering in exile, temperance was probably a thing of surpassing beauty, giving a person rectitude, balance, and style. Its key is control. Without some control, a passionate person who naturally goes to extremes is lost. So is any girl who wants to take command of her life. Temperance, then, in its many forms and different names, occupied a prominent niche in her school's curriculum.

It was not pointed out to her young students, though, that temperance can be a tyrant. For it decrees that even virtue carried to extremes can be a vice. That leaves room for the Dionysus thing—the occasional outbreak of wildness to let off steam; then, after one dizzily returns from a spree or gropingly crawls back from the world's edge after peering into the bottomless pit of nauseous chaos, one can contritely pray to his guardian deity and begin life again. By God's grace, a single lifetime is capable of infinite beginnings; otherwise, man is lost, for his judgments are too fallible.

Wisdom is an intellectual virtue, and it was Pittacus's forte. Kept off the playing fields by his physical deformity, and his spirit inflamed by the Renaissance, young Pittacus avidly pursued knowledge. That was before philosophy existed. Then poetry and mythology were in fullest bloom, and Ionians believed themselves to be superior to all other living things on earth and akin to the gods. That postulated divine relationship, working subjectively, repeatedly set higher goals for man to achieve and made Ionians, and subsequently all Greeks, unique. This prompted Oxford's late Prof. C. W. Bowra to observe: "Greek civilization was ultimately made possible by the belief in the special worth of man."

The most difficult thing for Pittacus to learn was that to be of any worth at all, he had to be a functioning member of society. Otherwise, he would be useless. And to be useless is to be worthless. Furthermore, to be fully functional he had to learn how to get along with the rowdies who had scoffed at his physical deformity and break into their circle of comradery. Then wisdom would have put him into possession of his enemy's stronghold, and he and they would cease to be enemies.

That pill of wisdom, bitter to ingest, started him on the long course of trying to understand the workings of human nature and, when judging a person, to try to balance a bad point with a good. It also started him to build up, methodically and grimly, his physical strength and agility so that, in due time, he could prove himself on the field of battle. This came about when he brought the war with Athens to a victorious end, for it was the custom to terminate peripheral wars, whenever mutually agreeable, by a combat of champions. And because *wisdom* in the Greek sense of the word meant practical knowledge, not esoteric knowledge dear to Eastern mystics, Pittacus was well equipped to be Mytilene's tyrant.

As tyrant, Pittacus's responsibilities were about the same, say, as those of a modern American president. For instance, his daily routine probably began with a session devoted to foreign affairs. That's where Mytilene's prosperity originated, and all of its peril. A follow-up of policies pursued abroad, either to counteract incipient trouble or to foster favorable developments, was essential. Bureaucratic implementation thereof had to be regularly checked, not overlooking a single point of responsibility; otherwise things soon got out of control and trouble ensued. With foreign-bound ships departing almost daily and with skippers and other trustworthy citizens aboard eager to serve Mytilene in any way, knowing diplomacy to be the first line of defense, and with capable ambassadors stationed at important royal palaces, Pittacus managed to stay on top of foreign affairs and not be dragged helplessly along by them.

Like a ship, a governmental machine best runs taut. With individual pride in a faultless performance and no idle busybodies cluttering things up, good teamwork finds daily satisfaction in achievement. Pittacus usually felt better after the day's opening session. He drew comfort from the team's hum and snap and was only rarely alarmed. Alarm, perhaps prompted by a faltering equivocation, always demands instant attention. And perhaps a serious amputation later on. Malfeasance is like a deadly social disease, for it quickly spreads when slyly aided by its henchman: untruthfulness. No foreign foe is more dangerous.

The daily session on foreign policy, seeking to cultivate good relations abroad and to obviate unpleasant surprises, was followed by its sibling: maritime affairs. It was comprised of such things as shipwrecks, attacks by pirates, salvage claims, fishing rights, and, quite often, pending additions and changes to the Law of the Sea, which were periodically enacted on Rhodes and recognized as valid by all Ionian city-states.

For Ionians, the Law of the Sea was a life-and-death matter. Legal regulations had to be extended to the great waters where they earned their living and not strictly confined to land, or havoc would ensue. It was difficult, however, because many countries were involved. A beginning was made when Ionia's ordinary maritime conventions, such as how ships should pass each other at sea when their courses converge, were persuasively conveyed to foreigners. Then a sailor's arms and a ship's bell learned to talk a simple language understood by barbarians as well as Greeks. Thus the Law of the Sea, born of necessity, found its initial home on Rhodes. There, where the cozy Aegean meets the Mediterranean and the world's busy trade routes converge, Ionia made the first foreign converts to its maritime practices.

Military affairs, always contentious, probably came next in Pittacus's daily routine. Even responsible generals succumb to the human tendency to relax in peacetime, and this can be dangerous. So call-ups to service, followed by a brief tactical exercise, periodically took place to test military readiness. Also, armaments fabricated by Mytilene's guilds of master craftsmen were routinely tested and inspected. Although citizens were obliged to equip themselves for military service, superiority of standard weapons could be assured only by official mandates. Ionian city-states vied for the best in arms. Each piece of armor, each weapon, had a standard that, in one way or another, was periodically raised. This always involved heated arguments, and much grumbling. But the trend to lighter arms continued, for it enhanced the troops' maneuverability and made them quicker and more deadly in close combat.

Pittacus also had to be sensitive to morale. The morale of the powerful slaves whose oar power propelled warships in lieu of wind, for instance, was as vital to victory as that of the maritime warriors trained to fight both on land and sea—Mytilene's most elite force.

In addition, it was always necessary to check pending military investigations, inspections, and reports. Are food reserves adequate? Is the lighter shield sufficiently tested against arrows? Against spears? Is the further shortening of swords warranted? Tempers sometimes flared, and arguments had to be cut short. Pittacus was always glad when it was over, but he had the satisfaction of knowing that his attention to humdrum military matters precluded unpleasant surprises.

The foregoing affairs of state grew out of Mytilene's economy, and their function was either to guide, nourish, or protect it. The economy was basic. It sustained life. It took up most of Pittacus's time. He would be held responsible if prosperity faded away and times got hard. That he knew. The worrisome question was how to prevent it.

Competition with other Ionian city-states was fierce. For Mytilene to drop behind in the quality of any export or auxiliary service rendered or stubbornly keep the price too high in a falling market, was self-defeating. That was Pittacus's gospel. He was forever preaching it to his fellow citizens.

The two mainstays of Mytilene's economy, wine and olive oil, were particularly vulnerable to price erosion. All city-states produced them. And bygone periods of oversupply, when price-cutting got out of hand, were painfully graven on everybody's memory. They were like long droughts, made grim by hunger. And if you didn't prudently save up in good years, how could you survive the bad? That's why Pittacus, believing civic finances to be the same as those of a private citizen, prudently used excess revenues to store up vital supplies, including gold itself, for the uncertain future.

After the day's work was over, Pittacus would hurry to his favorite wine garden to relax with friends and happily exercise his lubricated throat in choral song. The harmony they achieved, a perfect harmony it seemed to his insensitive ears, was something to marvel at. It surpassed all other forms of human cooperation, achieving perfection effortlessly, joyously. That's why Pittacus wanted to be part of it. Of course, being a realist, he realized that Mytilene's good wine had something to do with it. And also the joy of knowing the day's work was done.

Perhaps once a week the pleasant hour or so spent in the wine garden was followed by another favorite diversion—teaching a class of young men the full meaning of the cardinal virtues. For Pittacus, this provided another kind of liveliness and a stronger stimulation. The evening class had spirited discussions, students asked challenging questions, and class time flew. Pittacus had discovered that it was important to associate with different age groups. Youth, for instance, was always refreshing. The eager young minds exhibited innocence and health, affirming human nature's foundation of goodness. Or so Pittacus chose to believe.

Pittacus explained to them how wisdom, if left to herself alone, would patiently gather courage, temperance, and justice around her, as a hen gathers her chicks under her wings, for the cardinal virtues are naturally boon companions and should be lifelong helpmates.

After class, Pittacus walked homeward with his students, sharing their blithe spirits. They were carefree; almost penniless, they seemed to own the world. What gave them such joy? Love of life? A sense of expanding mental powers? Or just youth? Whatever it was, Pittacus wanted some of it, and to forget his own crushing ignorance. The more you learn, he had discovered, the more what you don't know looms larger and infinitely larger.

Justice is a social virtue. Although present in tribal societies, its full development didn't occur until it found warm wombs in city-states. There it had steady nourishment, plenty of exercise, and ceaseless demands. The Greek word *dike*, which we translate to be *justice*, initially denoted the boundaries of a man's land and metaphorically conveys the notion that he should keep within his own sphere and respect that of his neighbor. Because private spheres are more intimately meshed within a city's restricted confines than in open countryside, city folk have more sensitive and difficult relations than country folk. Justice's exacting task was properly to define those relationships.

Although city folk invited the imposition of law to make living together easier, aristocratic farmers, who had a sense of absolute ownership, were jealous of their rugged independence. They felt like local kings. That attitude made it psychologically difficult for them to compromise any right or to organize into guilds as craftsmen in the city did in order to promote their own interests, hence their sense of being victimized and the perennial rural complaint about the fickle marketplace. However, to embody justice in the law is not easy. "The most just law ever enacted by man," a Roman magistrate once declared, "cannot be enforced without inflicting, in some cases, total injustice."

To Plato, justice was the supreme virtue; to Socrates, wisdom was supreme. That Pittacus was elected and re-elected tyrant to obtain more justice for the rising bourgeois class there can be little doubt. And because he made justice the prime consideration of his regime, focusing upon it, agonizing over it, he was frustrated by the public's slow acceptance of new moral concepts. This, in turn, led to self-doubt. Was he losing his acumen? Was his judgment warped? If he was no longer politically effective, wasn't it time to leave office—leave it in orderly condition, with honor, while still in his prime? The question of abdication goaded him again, and with more urgency.

It is also truthful to say that Pittacus, for whom the golden years of youth were unknown, also wanted to enjoy, at long last, the good life. According to folklore, four things are indispensable to the good life: health, beauty, wealth, and to be young among friends; and they were valued in that order.

Obviously, health is indispensable. Without it, nobody can enjoy life. "To your health" was a customary Ionian toast. And although Ionians may not have known the beneficent effects of eating an apple a day, they were fond of apples, as their poets and artists depicted. Sappho, in a lovely poetic fragment, speaks of an apple on the topmost bough of a tree, too high for harvesters to pick, like a symbol of goodness everybody should reach for. Even Olympic gods, basking in eternal youth, were concerned with health. It was the particular province of Apollo, aided by Aesculapius and his daughter, Hygeia. They also came to the aid of mortals, who worshiped them.

Beauty, the good life's second most important attribute, meant, first of all, physical beauty. If something was beautiful, it couldn't be anything but good. That was Ionia's creed. Ugliness was evil. Poets, musicians, and artists found unfailing inspiration in beauty, perceiving in its depths the wonders of spiritual harmony. And if one lacked inward harmony, that spiritual deformity would eventually become manifest and remove him or her from the roster of the beautiful.

Health and beauty, basically twins, were divine gifts. The naked young men and well-clothed maidens that sculptors loved to create out of marble or bronze were virtually spiritualized flesh. Their noble characters were touched by the divine, and it showed.

Beauty in men was as highly valued as beauty in women, but it had to reflect capacity for action, thus serving the male function. Female beauty, too, must be more than skin-deep, suggesting the mystery of creation and the sanctity of motherhood. Simple carnality, such as that devoted to Aphrodite

126

Porne, was pictorially displayed only in brothels, or Palaces of Sweet Embrace, which, legend says, were evil opulences imported from Lydia.

The annual beauty contest in Mytilene, which Alcaeus briefly described, illustrates the religious sanction that beauty enjoyed. Conducted under the auspices of Hera's shrine, a family place of worship, it joyfully celebrated the coming of age of the girls best qualified to propagate the earth's most noble species.

That beauty is inherent in nature, abiding in both spirit and matter, was a Greek discovery. It was all that is good, seen and unseen. The Greeks wanted to consort with it, making it part of their lives. So beautiful cities they built, and they put beautiful things in their homes, and they clad their bodies attractively. Only in such a realm could justice hope to reign, making its spiritual beauty sovereign in the affairs of men.

Alas, Pittacus was not beautiful. His deformity was a serious handicap. As a youth, he was cruelly barred from the good life. He knew painful years. For him to withdraw from society and vent his spleen thereupon would have been normal. Instead, he sought solace in wisdom. The counsels of folklore were a balm. In due time, he gained mastery over himself.

Modern zealots may cite Pittacus as a powerful argument against the Ionian practice of infanticide. Unwanted babies were exposed to die at birth. If a child was one too many mouths to feed or had a serious defect, it was immediately given merciful death. That was better, Ionians apparently believed, than to risk having the child face a bleak life and an agonizing death later on. The parents who gave it life were the sole judge. That it was a heartrending decision goes without saying, that it was best for the child was assumed, and that it was a form of natural selection that improved Ionia's racial stock seems to have been borne out.

Pittacus, possibly the only child of an aristocratic couple able to support him, may have been desperately wanted. His physical defect, then, would have been disregarded. And the final result was a happy one. We should note, however, that the philosophers, the medical profession, and the religious leaders took no more exception to Ionia's method of population control than they did to slavery. And the modern world has yet to evolve a more effective way, or a more humane way, to control unlimited human propogation, with its resulting worldwide miseries.

Wealth was the third attribute of the good life. Without it, a man cannot really function. Destitution renders a man immobile, and it is degrading. To amass wealth beyond a golden mean, however, denotes a lack of wisdom, a spiritual deformity, or both. To have the means to enjoy life's simple felicities is enough, for they are forever new, forever fresh, and have inexhaustible depths.

Here Pittacus was right on target. His small estate had a vineyard and olive trees on hillsides, pasturage with cows, goats, and horses, vegetable and flower gardens, chickens, berry patches, and fruit trees. These afforded him a comfortable living. In addition, he probably had a share in a winery and perhaps also in a ceramics enterprise. That was it. That was his wealth before he became tyrant. That was all he would have after leaving office. He wasn't rich, but he had enough.

Contemplating his retirement, Pittacus looked forward to the leisure he would again enjoy as a country gentleman. And his gnawing self-doubts fell away as he reviewed his achievements as tyrant. He had started out to be a prudent ruler, to put the city's affairs in order. He had successfully resisted all attempts to make him spend lavishly on civic improvements and festivals. Human experience had clearly demonstrated that it was imperative to save for a rainy day. For it always comes, and sometimes comes with devastating suddenness, as in the case of a rampaging flood, an earthquake, an unexpected war. Well, Mytilene was in much better shape now. Storage bins were full of grain and also forage for livestock. Ingots of iron, copper, bronze, tin, silver, and gold made sizable stacks in the old hilltop fortress. And more men had jobs, homes and gardens of their own, and larders reasonably full. And they had the leisure to serve Mytilene in any way they chose, beyond their ordinary duties as citizens, such as military service.

To be young among friends was the fourth and final criterion of the good life. Here again, obviously, Pittacus failed. He was no longer young. It was made a criterion, Pittacus knew, because youth is when our capacity for enjoyment is at its peak, when life tingles with the freshness of daybreak and just to breathe is exhilarating. And in postulating the good life, Ionians naturally specified the best.

This criterion also indicated that Ionians abhorred old age. Mimnermus, lamenting that youth is menaced by the twin dooms of old age and death, declared old age the worst. And Euripides, more than a century later, voiced the same lament:

> Youth is always dear to me;
> Old age is a load that lies
> More heavily on the head
> Than the rocks of Etna.

Ionia's obsession with youth gradually subsided, however, after philosophers ushered in their revolutionary era. They persuasively demonstrated that the intellectual life was man's preeminent domain, that the mind's higher life had excitements, challenges, and achievements beyond the capacity of giddy youth to envision. Pittacus subscribed to that gospel. He was one of the first to help it achieve recognition. Hence Sophocles, who was still writing plays when he was ninety years old, could say:

> The wise never grow old
> Their minds are nursed by living
> With the holy light of day.

Pittacus, finally abdicating with no illusions about his prospects for the good life, was yet full of illusions. He would serve his beloved Mytilene as a private citizen in any way he could and also, he believed, capture some of the golden moments he had missed as a youth. Sappho, for instance, had always fascinated him. He had never really known her. But as his bitter opponent in the election campaign she had seemed the essence of femininity, charming even in her most scolding moods.

The two poets would soon have their separate homecomings. They would be private affairs, restricted to their families and closest friends, with no official ceremonies. That had already been decided. Afterward Pittacus would pay Sappho a formal visit and proffer his friendship, fervently hoping she would accept it.

Even in wintertime, when the north wind is cold and nasty, Pittacus preferred having breakfast in an outdoor bower in front of his house. There, on a high terrace, he would look down on the ever-changing sea, the changeless sea, and gather strength to help him face the many problems of the day just breaking, with Apollo rising and spectacularly routing darkness with his imperial shafts of brilliance and color.

Ships on the sea always made the view more fascinating. And usually there were several, either approaching or leaving

Mytilene, their sails sometimes belly full, tautly tacking, or struck. "A host of ships is the most beautiful thing, some say, on the face of the dark earth." That line by Sappho must have often come to Pittacus's mind as he watched, and now he wondered if one of the inbound ships was bringing either Sappho or Alcaeus home, for their estimated time of arrival was overdue.

Pittacus broke off surveying the seascape for his usual early morning romp with his favorite goat. Winter's precious greenery, patiently gathered every day from nearby stream beds, was kept in a box on the terrace, with the goat waiting expectantly beside it. Only heavy stones on the box kept the goat from pushing the lid open and feasting. When Pittacus opened the box and snatched out a big handful of wild grass and weeds, their diurnal game began. Holding it high, Pittacus capered about, with the goat leaping for a succulent mouthful. Both were agile and quick, but the goat was more so. Then fetching another tempting handful, Pittacus cavorted and twisted so fast it was impossible to believe that he was lame. Indeed, he had acquired a dexterity and fluidity of movement he never had before. And when he abruptly stopped, handful of greenery held triumphantly high, he had a regal poise that only a Greek dancer can attain. Watching him was the old slave heating his gruel on the glowing brazier in the vine-clad, leafless bower, her face crinkling with smiles.

The lively sport was interrupted by the arrival of a runner who, a little breathlessly, told Pittacus that Sappho had arrived. She was on a ship that had docked in the night. And already word had spread and people were gathering on the bayfront. The news brought pandemonium to Pittacus's small household. His other slaves quickly came together on the terrace, as if an alarm had sounded. Pittacus dispatched one of them to the cool cellar to fetch a large basket of fruit and nuts, decorated with laurel, to be taken to town as a welcoming gift. Pittacus was elated. The others, however, were not. "Why so glum?" Pittacus asked them. "This is a big day for Mytilene."

The eldest male slave, superintendent of the farm, finally spoke up: "Have you forgotten, Master? Sappho is your enemy—our enemy."

"You cannot step into the same river twice." The reality of that gnomic saying of Heracleitus is a bitter pill to swallow for anyone coming home after a long absence. So it was with Sappho and Alcaeus. Their homecomings by ship, separated by less than a week, were dramatic events, noisy with welcoming fanfare, for they were still Mytilene's best known public figures and apparently much beloved. Droves of common people were there, for it was impossible to exclude them. On this first reception for Sappho, for instance, the people on the edge of the crowd, the latecomers, were not pushy. They seemed content just to be there. They had come primarily to pay their respects and were all smiles, saying to each other, "It's good to have her home."

In the crowd's epicenter, though, things were different. The tearful meeting of Sappho with her family and old friends, greedy with embraces and kisses, was a choked-up affair, inarticulate, for a sudden flood of emotion cannot be put into words, although straining silence to bursting. Sobbing was the usual emotional release, and it created a hush in the bystanders. Heads bowed and tears were shed in sympathy.

But soon, all too soon, Sappho regained her senses and discovered that Mytilene was not the same. People were not the same. Little things had changed; everything had changed. And she slowly realized that she did not quite fit into her old special niche of everyday life, that the roseate bloom was gone, and her heart ached for more intimacy with her family, which wasn't there, which had never really been there, and her spirit reached out for something solid to grasp, to sustain her, to help her find her bearings into the future.

Pittacus called upon her and was graciously received. They were both shy like children, uncertain of what to say or do, until Pittacus made a forthright speech, declaring that he would be honored if she would allow him to call upon her occasionally and serve her in any way he could. Time would likely be kind to them, he told her, helping them to know each other better. She was flattered by the offer, she replied, saying the high wall of enmity between them must be mutually breached and that she would do her part.

"Ah, that is good news!" Pittacus said. "Thank you! Now I am sure we'll get on very well. I must also tell you that I'm here in an official capacity. I am a special envoy of Dion, our new tyrant. He welcomes you home on behalf of all our citizens and sends you every best wish for the future. He has also appointed you patroness of the Festival of Aphrodite. That is less than three weeks away. Dion fervently hopes that you will accept."

Listening to him, Sappho's enigmatic smile had become radiant. "That is good of him," she said. "Very good. Thank him for me, please. Thank him very much."

"Then you accept?"

"It is a great honor. I am happy to accept."

"Now I must ask an official favor," Pittacus said. "It is on behalf of all citizens, not just Dion and myself. You are aware, I presume, that this is an Olympic year."

Sappho said she was aware of it.

Then Pittacus related the desperate plight of Mytilene's contestants—all of them, both individuals and teams. And

133

he stressed the short time remaining before the major spring festivals and then the Olympics. "There must be someone in Mytilene who can break through their paralyzing depression," Pittacus said, "and arouse them to normal life again." He stopped pacing the room. "Well," he said, confronting her, "Dion and I have talked it over many times. We believe that someone is you."

Sappho had been listening with a rapt expression. Now she met his gaze and held it. Then she reached to the nearby tripod table, picked up a bell, and rang it. A slave appeared. Sappho asked the elderly woman if any old ruby wine was still left in the cellar. The slave thought there was and was sent to fetch it. "There is so little time," Sappho said, as if speaking to no one.

"I know," Pittacus said.

Sappho was lost in reverie. "The best dance and choral teams are always selected at the Festival of Aphrodite," she said, fondly reminiscing. "They are beautiful to watch, beautiful to listen to. They teach us how life ought to be."

Pittacus said nothing.

"Those young people have been training since early childhood," Sappho continued. "All their fundamental skills are in place. They know how to work together. It is only a matter of spirit."

Pittacus kept watching her changing expressions.

"It is sometimes difficult to reach the spirit," she said. "Terribly difficult. Moods, especially the awful mood of depression, can be stubborn. Maddeningly stubborn! It tends to lock itself in. And hold on and on, like a winter's fire smoldering and smoldering."

Pittacus broke the following silence. "You reach the spirit better than anyone alive. Your poetry is a heart speaking to other hearts."

The slave returned. She was carrying a tray with a carafe and two goblets. Sappho told her to leave it on the table, that she would pour. She got up from the sofa when the slave left and began filling a goblet. "When can we start?" she asked. "There is no time to lose."

"Tomorrow," Pittacus said. "Arrangements have already been made. I hope you will forgive my presumption."

She gave him a goblet of wine. "Forgiven," she said. She filled the other goblet and, following the usual custom, touched it lightly to his. "To victory," she said.

So began a tumultuous fortnight. Pittacus escorted Sappho to the various training groups and she addressed them in ringing words. Afterward she mingled with them like a loving comrade who had been long absent, and they got on wondrously, for her sincerity was manifest. Her personality, indeed, bloomed. All her talents were called upon. The role fit her perfectly. Her emotional rapport with the dance and choral teams was particularly quick and strong. With them, laughter and tears alternated naturally, making words largely superfluous. After each exhausting day, Pittacus took Sappho to a wine garden to relax. There they would eat, drink, talk, sit in thoughtful silence, and try to find enjoyment.

Pittacus chose only small, out-of-the-way wine gardens where some privacy was possible. Sappho was the only woman present. Times were changing, Pittacus told her, so they might as well help the new trend. Nowadays young couples, male and female, were going to large, popular wine gardens and sort of taking them over. It was noisy there and restless. Young people wanted only excitement. Here, of course, in an old-fashioned, all-male province, Sappho and Pittacus were conspicuous. They were prominently set apart not only by their uniqueness and fame, but also by the fact that they were former enemies, bitter enemies. That puzzled the other patrons. They discussed it in hushed voices.

At first, Sappho was tense. She couldn't unwind immediately. She kept mentioning faults in individuals, in teams, and in coaches. And the important things she should have done but didn't. And the many pressing things waiting to be done. The success or failure of all contestants, their whole future, Mytilene's future, were now her responsibility. Obviously, Sappho had assumed a staggering burden.

After a few days, Pittacus tried to slow her down. Maybe her daily schedule was too full, he said. That was his mistake of course. Now her schedule should be cut a little. He'd call for her later in the morning, and she must have decent intervals of rest in the day. He'd . . . Sappho cut him short. She'd have none of it. There weren't enough hours of daylight as it was. Who can rest when things need urgently to be done? Olympic championships, particularly in the arts that she dearly loved, had to come back to Mytilene. That was her sole ambition now. It commanded all her strength, all her thoughts. Well, not quite all. For suddenly she smiled at Pittacus. It was a charming smile. She was a banquet woman again. A gay companion. And her laughter was like music.

They went to a different wine garden every evening. It was always a small and select place, remote from pedestrian traffic. They were like adolescents exploring life together for the first time, finding diversion in each new adventure. One evening, though, their faces were drawn. They seemed more emotionally drained than usual. Had they quarreled? As soon as they were seated and the obsequious proprietor had left and the fluttering waitresses had served them and had withdrawn to just within peeking distance, Sappho placed a hand on Pittacus's arm. "We see things differently, don't we?" she said. "I suppose I should always give way to you, but I can't. Georgias must go. We need a new singing coach. Parrhasius is the best. He should be given the post tomorrow."

136

"That will be done," Pittacus said.

"Oh, thank you," Sappho said, her face lighting up. "I wouldn't ask if there was any other way. You know that, don't you?"

"I know," Pittacus said. "I point out only considerations of which you may not be fully aware—matters of procedure, citizens' rights, important things like that. Of course you and I are different. That's an advantage. You operate by intuition; I try to operate by reason. This is a time for intuition to be in command. That I know. In return, I ask only two favors: First, whenever another citizen's rights are involved, always consult me before making a decision. Second, please, Sappho, don't drive yourself so hard. Slow down! You are killing yourself." They smiled at each other then and began to eat and drink. The other patrons who had been covertly watching them did likewise.

Wine garden gossip, in point of fact, kept fully abreast of what was going on in the gymnasia and on the training fields. And it was remarkably accurate. The moods and spirits of the contestants as well as their daily accomplishments were eagerly shared that evening by the whole citizenry. Everything was humming beautifully now in all arenas of training, and progress was phenomenal. As a result, patrons began getting to their feet when Pittacus and Sappho entered a wine garden and cheered them. Some brought small gifts to their table to show their appreciation. One evening, in presenting a bouquet of blossoming willows, the garden's proprietor made a little speech, saying the city's gloom was rapidly being replaced by good cheer—a very welcome good cheer. Finally, at last, citizens were smiling. They had a year of championships to look forward to.

Sappho and Pittacus were dismayed. This sudden acclaim, this public optimism, was unexpected. Their minds were riveted on shortcomings of the contestants, on minor faults unnoticed by ordinary observers, but nonetheless real, and very serious. "This is the worst thing that could happen to us," Sappho said, her emotions rising. "Smug satisfaction! Don't you see? It's poison! The contestants will absorb it! They can't help but absorb it. It will ruin them. We must do something!" She fell silent. It was an ominous silence. "Tomorrow," she continued in a determined voice, "if they are not true children of a spring evening, if each movement doesn't have verve and spontaneity, I'll scream at them! I'll scream and scream! I'll be a Fury! I'll teach them not to tolerate merely the good. Tomorrow belongs to Dionysus. It belongs to the disordered wildness out of which perfection is born." She drained her goblet and held it out for Pittacus to refill. "Please," she said, "you must stand back of me, Pittacus. You must help me. We can't fail now."

"You are a perfectionist," Pittacus said calmly, taking her goblet and starting to refill it. "That always worries me. If you push these young people too fast, just a little too fast, or too far, they'll explode. You know that, don't you?" He placed her goblet before her and started filling his own. "Go ahead and scream at them tomorrow. Scream and scream and scream. And I'm sure you'll explain in advance precisely what fault must be corrected, and with all the different individuals and teams you'll have many fine decisions to make, crucial decisions. These youngsters, don't forget, are now living on their nerves as you are. Their temperaments are fragile. So the risk is very, very great."

"We don't have any choice, do we?" Sappho said. "We either win or we lose. To be champions, you must risk everything. That's what I intend to do."

"That makes sense if, and only if, you keep within the bounds of human nature. You know these youngsters better than anyone else, so I'm betting on you." He lifted his goblet. "Here's to Dionysus." They touched goblets and drank. "Hungry?" Pittacus asked.

"I'm not in the least bit hungry."

"Well, anyway, let's have some of these," he said, pulling over a small dish heaping with walnuts, pecans, and pistachios and another dish of fat, green olives and another of small, black, wrinkled olives and another of pickled fish in lime juice and another of boiled eggs sprinkled with paprika, and another with slices of cold fowl and pork and another with sliced pickled cucumber and another with wedges of octopus braised with garlic. "Oom," Pittacus intoned. "This octopus is delicious. Try it." He watched her eat a wedge and apparently agree. "We'll have one more goblet of wine—just one more. Then I'm taking you home. We'll both need a good night's rest."

Fatigue was more deeply graven on their faces the following evening, but they appeared to be at peace with themselves. They were making their way on a stone-lined path along a narrow seafront. They walked slowly, as if time didn't matter. The quietude that engulfed them seemed like a god-given spiritual armor, protecting them. They were going to one of Pittacus's favorite cafés. It was in a secluded cove, a rendezvous for mermaids, legend says. Breaking with his habit of choosing a café at the last moment, Pittacus had sent word ahead to expect them. Today was special. The only thing in their demeanor to indicate the day's unique importance, though, was a certain lassitude, as if all strength had been drained from them.

Torchlight illuminated the café when they arrived. A table in the front row had been reserved for them. It was decorated with a bouquet of early spring blossoms, and the latticework in front of the café was festooned with ferns. Beyond was the cove with its rocky headlands and the usual lineup of sea gulls waiting expectantly. A colorful array of foodstuffs was on the table, occupying about a dozen small bowls and dishes. At Sappho's request, the two chairs were placed close together so they could both sit facing the sea. As soon as they were seated, Sappho began inspecting the tempting tidbits that had been placed before them. She was delighted. "This is one of my favorites!" she exclaimed. "And here is another!" She looked searchingly at Pittacus, long and hard. "Now I remember," she said. "This afternoon, late this afternoon, you asked me what my favorite appetizers were. I pleaded with you not to bother me. But you kept asking. So I told you." Abruptly she buried her face into a fold of her tunic and wept. Pittacus put his arm around her. A waitress coming to their table with a round loaf of freshly baked, partially sliced bread was disconcerted. Pittacus told her to leave the bread on the table and resumed speaking softly to Sappho, trying to comfort her. "Then I knew you would not only survive, but triumph," Pittacus said. "That all of us would triumph. You were a terrible Fury. You were also a marvelous human being. And perhaps, thinking about it now, we should admit, in all honesty, without detracting one whit from your superb performance, that Dionysus was very kind to us."

Sappho looked up then, sniffing. "That bread has a delicious aroma," she said. She wiped the tears from her eyes and noticed the mascara on her linen handkerchief. "We used to call this the Egyptian color," she said. "But in Lydia they call it the Lesbian shadow. Really, we have an excellent reputation abroad. So many of the best things come from here. Lydians admit that we do more things better than anybody else. But if we ever stop doing things better and better and better the whole situation will drastically change. And for the worst." She broke off a small chunk of bread, dipped it in the lime juice and olive oil covering fish in a small bowl, and munched it. "Hm-m-m, hm-m-m," she intoned, lifting her eyes heavenward. "I'm starved!"

They fell to eating then, and with gusto. After each bite, each sampling of a different appetizer, they sipped wine to enhance the savor. And for the first time in a long while their stomachs became kings of their bodies, calling forth vital juices of well-being, old and familiar sentiments, and private thoughts not for utterance. Now, finally, they could envision the success ahead of them and it was exciting. Mytilene would revel in championships! Also, it was a tremendous relief to escape the crushing responsibility that had been theirs for so many demanding, hectic days—precious days, for they were always fighting against time. Yes, the worst was over. But it was also sad. For it meant the end of an absorbing job. It was a gratifying job, a job that had brought them together and that had commanded all of their energies. Would this relationship, this precious relationship, also end? Or wouldn't it be better, actually, to terminate it? It was too much! It was too overwhelming! This wonderful companion, this irreplaceable companion, brought only excitement, but not peace —excitement with its feverish restlessness, its abrasive achievements, its brittle gaity, but not the surcease of peace—beautiful peace with its balm of rest and the ineffable sweetness of fulfillment. Isn't that life's highest reward? And aren't those rewards periodically needed for life to be tolerable?

Such thoughts fitfully preoccupied Sappho's and Pittacus's minds as they greedily ate, occasionally talked, and laughingly tossed hunks of bread to the quickly darting and squawking sea gulls in the penumbra of torchlight. This relationship was something new to them. They had never been involved like this before. Now, suddenly, their personal fates loomed urgently. This new anxiety, this hidden anxiety, however, was abruptly interrupted. Three muscular young men

141

and a statuesque matron came to their table, stopped, and respectfully bowed. They were handsome fellows and painfully shy. The eldest of them carried a wicker basket, and after a few stumbling words he spoke well, saying that he and his brothers were members of Mytilene's wrestling team. They were grateful to Pittacus and Sappho for rescuing them and many, many more from black despondency, all of them sinking in a terrible psychic shipwreck. As a token of their gratitude, they had brought fish from their father's catch on a voyage just ended. Then the impressive matron spoke up, saying she and her husband were eternally grateful to Sappho. Their sons had been strictly reared to be worthy citizens. They had also been reared to be champions. But today Sappho did what their parents were unable to do. She shook them up. She shamed them for being too easily satisfied. She shamed them for falling short of what they could do. Of what they must do. Or else, fail. Fail after training so long and so faithfully. Fail and bring shame upon the city!

The silence following the matron's brief recital was filled only by the swish and rattle of waves on the rocky shore. Then Pittacus, accepting the fish, thanked them profusely on behalf of Sappho and himself. Shortly afterward, they, too, rose to depart, leaving unfinished a mélange of fruit preserves with a dash of brandy and several honey cakes. The café's other patrons, a mixture of city folk and fishermen, also rose to their feet out of respect. They seemed like the human family, obeying its own ritual as the earth's nobility. And the eternal beat of the waves on the dark shore was another voice of creation, saying nature never rests but is always changing, becoming something it has never been before. And the moonlight and starlight, following Sappho and Pittacus home, illuminated the way, helping to fill the night with its myriad media of communication and power, practically all of them beyond the ability of human senses to discern, but within the ken of wisdom and intuition, which someday may discover and utilize them much more fully than now. The two greatest practitioners of wisdom and intuition in that day and age, however, were engaged not in logical speculation or in flights of poetic fancy. They were thinking about their own earthly fates, whether they should be together or apart.

For the first time, Sappho entertained Pittacus to dinner the following evening. It was held in the school's courtyard, which looked elegant with its tilework, fountain, and shrubbery. Some students played lyres; others formed a chorus and sang. They were shy and excited and looked very pretty. And the harmony of their voices was pleasant to hear. Everybody seemed as happy as the first birds of spring, for lilac blossoms filled the courtyard with fragrance, the two adults had had another rewarding day on the training fields, and the Festival of Aphrodite was just two days away.

As was the custom, Sappho began pouring wine to proffer the introductory toast. She gave the first chalice to Pittacus. As she filled the second chalice, though, her hand shook, and she dropped it. The spilled wine overflowed the table and stained the wool rug on the mosaic floor—the luxuriant white and purple-bordered rug from Lydia. The singing faltered. Slaves hurried forward to clean up the mess. And Sappho and Pittacus, disconcerted, may have recalled the old adage: "Spilled wine is neither thine nor mine, but the devil's or God's." And it may have seemed a portent, saying not to overstep the limits of friendship, not to dream foolish dreams, but to thy own nature be true. Perhaps Pittacus, to end the embarrassment, poured wine into a fresh chalice, gave it to Sappho, and, with his wry humor, proffered his own toast: "To whatever the future holds for us, may it always be benign, or weaker than we are."

Despite those hopeful words, disengagement was the process that both of them realized they had to follow. They had to break off their relationship to a degree of friendship that was sustainable. And they had to do so without affront, without violating good manners, and with no hurt to the other, if possible.

Breaking off any relationship, however, is not without pain. And when two people realize they need each other, perhaps need each other desperately, the pain can be severe. But Sappho and Pittacus knew that a limit had been reached, that further intimacy between them was impossible.

Following Sappho's unfortunate dinner, the spring holiday began. It is the year's first big holiday, born of the venerable seedtime ritual of olden days, but now refined to purge winter's rheums, aggravations, and glooms and to usher in spring's felicities. The Festival of Aphrodite is its vibrant heart, transforming everybody's life with renewed significance and excitement.

All training in athletics and the arts is suspended. Everybody is free to attend the festival every day and have a whole day's rest beforehand. Even so, three days are hardly enough to take in everything the festival has to offer. And such variety! There are merchants with their exotic wares from Babylonia, Assyria, Phoenicia, and other foreign lands. And chariot races. And sideshows, some of them featuring famous belly dancers from Egypt. And roving singers, tumblers, and acrobats building living pyramids. And of course wild horsemen from the Crimea.

The festival's real excitement, though, is the elimination contest of the dance and choral teams. That's the main feature. People rarely meet without exchanging gossip about the teams and voicing their hopes and expectations. And also their disappointment when a favorite team is eliminated. Some dejected fans, indeed, go to Sappho for commiseration.

144

They weep together. And, before the fans leave, Sappho manages to cheer them up, citing the winning team's excellence, something about which all Mytilene can be proud.

As patroness, Sappho looks lovely and strikingly regal in her long white gown. Surrounded by pretty handmaidens, her court is always open. Formal receptions are held several times each day, however, to keep things orderly, for Sappho is more than a figurehead. She is very much a part of the invisible machinery that keeps the festival's diverse activities functioning smoothly and on schedule. She has little spare time. The festival's real chief, though, is a professional bard from Chios; a master showman, he confers with her daily, and between times they keep in touch by messengers. Unexpected things always happen, requiring quick coordination and adjustments in timing. Nevertheless, everything proceeds at a lively pace with gradually increasing excitement. Then all spectators are brought to their feet at the rousing finale. And soon they are wildly cheering, for the winning dance and choral teams execute the grand strophe as a flirtatious twosome and then intricately and joyously weave themselves together and triumphantly merge into one. It is nerve-tingling! It is sensational! It is as deeply satisfying as nature's mysterious and comforting song about eternal truth being changeless, but only garbed in perpetual change. Everybody is wildly elated.

Well, not quite everyone. Sappho doesn't appear to be happy. Standing on the patroness's dais, she seems distraught. She keeps looking nervously around. Finally, she spots Pittacus, whose eyes are on her. They wave exuberantly to each other with their faces lit up. Then she reluctantly turns back and acknowledges the cheers from the throng.

Afterward, Sappho continues her dawn to darkness busyness. She works with other teams and individuals in their daily training, meets regularly with her literary circle, and scrupulously performs her many duties at school, forever seeking perfectability in each pupil, the ghost of love hovering.

Now the popular wine gardens are full after nightfall. Torchlight plays on happy faces, for spring is intoxicating. And love songs, in addition to the usual drinking songs, punctuate the festivities with something brazenly new. Talk is lively. It's mostly about Mytilene's dance and choral teams, which seem to be the best ever. Everyone expects them to win the all-Greek contests this summer. Then the coveted trophies of the most popular arts will return to the acropolis and occupy their usual place of honor. That's where they belong. For this is Mytilene, capital of the arts and music's home.

The love songs that rise above the chatter and laughter and ultimately snuff them out prompt a mixed reception. Listening to them, some young people seem puzzled, others embarrassed or mildly shocked, a few rapt. Apparently, this is something that people are not used to. To make private feelings and secret yearnings public is not validated by custom. It is daring. It is shameless. They concern only the people involved, whether rustic adolescents hopelessly smitten by Eros's arrows, a moon-dazed maiden at her barred window, or an errant prince with his illicit philandering. In any case, they are trivial. They can't be compared to legitimate drinking songs, songs about community affairs, songs about life's significant happenings, such as maidenhood, marriage, and death.

The rendering of love songs seems to be impulsive. Both aristocrats and commoners, given the right to sing, voice the old complaints of the heart. Most people know these secret pains and joys, having experienced them themselves, but they have kept them private or divulged them only to close friends.

Nonetheless, people listen to them avidly. Many of them thrill to the emotional adventures or misadventures. Older people are either particularly pleased or shocked. Many of them welcome the new openness, saying it is simple honesty. Moreover, they are comforted by the emotional companionship. They don't want it to stop. Reflecting the truth of the old adage "Misery loves company," they don't want to be alone.

Nevertheless, love songs are not easy to accept. Some are like a person undressing in public, standing naked, and exposing a wounded soul. Most of them are shamefully self-centered, vain, and pathetic. But they are also very satisfying to listen to. The audience keeps clamoring for more.

But already, within the eyelash flicker of a single lifetime, people are forgetting who sponsored this new fashion in song, this vocal comradery of love's open confessional, this emotional democracy of male and female, partners in biological reproduction, both hopelessly stricken from puberty to old age by the imperative urge to reproduce, until some distraught victims finally rebel and try to voice, perhaps shrilly voice, their personal plight in love's throes.

Love's infinite variety is boundless, and its poetic discoveries will never end. And whether passionately rampant and hotly receptive, dewy soft as a baby's kiss, or the solitary glory of laying down one's life for a stranger, love's loyal servitude deserves a song.

To begin with, though, this new field of artistic endeavor had to be opened by a poetic genius, one who would boldly explore its full range of emotions, savoring its pains and ecstasies and then placing them, distilled into poetry, as a humble offering on the altar of beauty, a sort of eternal bouquet to the only thing human that may be more than transitory.

The fascinating subject of love, vocally enthroned by poetry's queen, was thus made ready for public obeisance.

In fulfilling that function, Sappho sang from a pinnacle of fame that carried her voice to the ends of the Greek world. And her lyrical gospel passionately proclaimed that love is the greatest thing in life.

And now Sappho, home at last and bereft of love, would go often alone to the bayfront at night and stay there for hours, gazing intently at the tender embrace of the moonlight and water, gently undulating together in perfect harmony, an exquisite intimacy of earth and moon, and she yearned for that golden rapture, that kiss of peace. And feverishly she would conjure up other images of beauty, trying to fit the melodic sounds in her ears to her heart's throb, knowing that lonely is the way until love finds its home and the daughters of music weep no more.

Afterward, alone in her room at school, unable to sleep, she would pluck her lyre and sing out those moonlit promises, evoking beautiful human rhapsodies, her voice rising to ecstatic triumph over the flooding tears from the old torment. And happily she would go to bed, believing that it was the end of sorrows.

And more than she knew, it was indeed an end. It was the end of Ionia's poetic era; it was the end of the Western world's beginning.

Sappho and Alcaeus were the last great Lesbian poets. With their passing, Lesbos lost its preeminence in music. Pittacus, one of the last beneficent tyrants, was commemorated about twelve generations later when coins were struck in Mytilene honoring him, and coins were also struck honoring Sappho, linking them together as the bygone civic leaders most worthy of veneration.

Sappho had many female imitators down through the years, but none was memorable. In Mytilene, too, philosophy eventually relegated poetry to the background, making it a bygone fashion. Aristotle, coming to Mytilene to do research in marine biology, founded a school and taught there, married Pythia, a native girl of the aristocracy, who gave him children and with whom he lived happily. It was from Mytilene that Philip II, king of Macedon, summoned Aristotle to instruct his headstrong son.

Aristotle and Alexander! Those quintessential exemplars of the Greek Renaissance changed the world enormously, but not always in ways agreeable to the other. Alexander, by extending his empire over three continents, rendered the miniature city-state, beloved by Aristotle, obsolescent. And Alexander's shining example of one man's astounding capability revived people's faith in kingships, so that kings, even today, are commonplace.

Most of all, Alexander's pervasive and enduring charisma and the cultural infrastructure he bequeathed to the Near East, particularly the Greek language, paved the way for the Roman Empire. Christianity grew up in the empire's far-reaching freedom—its most precious Greek inheritance. Alexander's hopeful inauguration of the brotherhood of man, however, was premature. And his attempted implementation thereof in his vast bureaucracy and armed forces caused much acrimonious trouble, particularly with his hard-core Macedonian veterans who fiercely resented Persian battalions and other Eastern soldiery having prerogatives and a pay scale equal to their own. This festering controversy added sourness to Alexander's final year.

How much influence did Aristotle, as tutor, have on the world's greatest conqueror? A satisfactory answer to that hoary question would require a Michelangelo accurately to depict the Western world's creation with divine power working through humans. In any case, for young Alexander, who had already selected Achilles to be his model, to acquire the steadfast habits of painstaking analysis, logical thinking, and functional organization was a peerless maturation for a military genius. One manifestation of Aristotle's influence is easily recognizable: the contingent of scholars Alexander took along on his Asian campaign to analyze, classify, and report on all unusual things encountered there. About two millennia later, Napoléon followed that example on his Egyptian campaign, to the laudation of France's academic community.

Aristotle remained at Pella, the Macedonian capital, until Alexander impatiently started his military career by brilliantly commanding his father's right wing against a Greek alliance led by Thebes, and then he returned to Mytilene. There, perhaps reading Sappho's poetry to appease his omnivorous mental hunger and finding inspiration in her felicitous evocation of beauty, he called her "the Tenth Muse." From Mytilene, Aristotle returned to Athens and reestablished his Lyceum in a sylvan suburb where he could teach while strolling in the shade of arching trees; hence his pupils were called "Peripatetics," which is an apt name, for philosophy was to know no boundaries.

Plato's Academy and Aristotle's Lyceum, heirs to Miletus's School of Philosophy, are prototypes of the West's universities. Their first offspring, Soter Ptolemy's collegiate library in Alexandria, was really a university, too. Its library, however, systematically collected by the Ptolemies, was its prime attraction to scholars and its abiding mystique. Even after fire consumed three centuries of accumulated knowledge, its resident scholars continued to function as a faculty with the whole Mediterranean world for a student body. Again, an oral tradition carried on until invaluable things of the mind could be put back into written words. And all the while Alexandria's vibrant heart, its treasure trove of books, or the memory thereof, was brought to life by resident scholars. They continued to promulgate and elucidate Greek culture, and its luminosity reached to the ends of the Western world. What university has done more?

Indeed, the Western world was stronger culturally than it was militarily. Although Western nations—Spain, Portugal, Great Britain, et al.—initially imposed their cultures on conquered peoples by force of arms, the West's culture spread primarily because of its recognized superiority. It was frequently sought, and its most desired features were systematically adopted.

The Western world is now global. Comprised of nation-states rather than city-states, it is restricted neither by geography nor race nor language. Membership is solely a matter of basic culture. That was decided at law long ago in Ionia.

Liberty's clarion call, of men striving to solve mutual problems while seeking self-fulfillment in their separate ways, either selfishly or unselfishly, and thereby helping individual talent to function at its best, is what holds the West together. That is its heart, its soul, its mystique.

The West's culture is pliable and therefore wondrously adaptable and strong. It is being molded every day in Stockholm and Singapore, say, and also in Rome, London, Berlin, Buenos Aires, Sydney, New York, and Tokyo. It is the blue jeans on young people in Oslo and Hong Kong, pop music, the Argentine tango, and bohemian life on the West Bank in Paris, the People's Court and St. Sophia in Istanbul, and all the religions of the world being practiced in Los Angeles.

The West's culture blends differently in each community. People either accept or reject any aspect of it. Local pressures to conform socially and laws mandating order are the only constraints. The whole Western world, some say, is gradually being homogenized by telecommunications, but so far, happily, not without beguiling nuances of local color.

Like the good old days in Ionia, Western nations are now engaged in fierce economic competition. With much social pain, older industrial nations have witnessed the demise of some of their largest industries. Industrial newcomers, such as Japan, Korea, and Taiwan, using Western technology and with lower pay scales and standards of living, undersell the old-timers even in their domestic markets. Serious unemployment has been engendered thereby, and it threatens to be chronic. Such critical problems may tax the ingenuity of the West's leaders for a long, long time. A free world and free market are inseparable. If its members cannot trade together to their mutual advantage, the West will disintegrate.

The governance of freedom is never easy. That's painfully true now in the former USSR, where the collapse of dictatorship and sudden pursuit of openness and freedom with food supplies dangerously low and a huge army being demobilized fosters counterrevolutions in order to survive with something in the belly.

The domestic relations of the various republics will probably remain restive and changeable for decades. So the whole world, not only the former Soviet Union, faces a lot of uncertain tomorrows.

Some people are optimistic. They envision a global marketplace that would keep factories humming everywhere to meet enormous demand. Financing? Oh, well, now that you mention it, that's still to be worked out.

Other optimists believe the West is now in another Renaissance, the world's third Renaissance. Many wonders, they say, will soon ensue. To support this belief, they cite the explosion of science that has taken place since the first atomic bombs brought Japan to its knees, such as the ongoing exploration of outer space and the exploration of infinitely minute antimatter, which merges with energy within the infinitesimal atom—the same atom that the Ionians had hypothesized. Science has accomplished more in the last forty years, its apologists say, than in any previous millennium. In any case, the modern buzzword is *science*. That's all that young people seem to have faith in. And young people are the future.

Well, to begin with, we'll probably have to wait a century or so in order to adjudge if this is a genuine Renaissance. Second, science is merely a tool of the human spirit. Only the spirit commands. Actually, we might be better off to heed someone like Pittacus, who, in Sappho's time, a time of song, strove to make justice the crowning glory of our culture.

So our quest must continue. To travel repeatedly along the well-blazoned trail of Western culture to its beginning, traversing the highs and lows of civilization, should be more than an intellectual enrichment. Someplace along the way we may catch helpful glimpses into the imperceptible relationship of the spiritual and physical realities. That, I believe, is still the most challenging aspect of the future, and potentially the most rewarding.

Today Mytilene has little to recall its golden youth. Old olive trees still flash silver-green when the inland breeze blows, and jagged hills boldly stand sentinel behind the modern city that curves gently around a placid bay, with a broad esplanade on the waterfront.

Viewed from the sea, the civic panorama is grand. In its center, though, two neon signs atop nearby buildings, proclaiming Hotel Sappho and Hotel Lesbos, appear garishly out of place, as if hustling business in unseemly fashion.

On close inspection, the hotels have a subdued atmosphere of faded elegance; they also have distinction. Paint is peeling from facades, the upholstery of the furniture in the lobbies is worn and frayed, and vintage elevators noisily complain when forced to go up or down. Of more importance, though, both hotels exude a spectral dignity that is charming. Even an American bar, popular with Mytilene's younger set at cocktail hour, cannot eradicate the ghostly presence. It is impossible not to suspect, for instance, that most of their patrons are still Victorian gentry, secure in a tidy world of aristocratic preferment, who quietly move unobtrusively through the lobby, trailing a scent of lavender to vanquish the faint odor of decay.

The whole town, in fact, has a dowdiness that comes from prolonged hard times. Trade with the Asian mainland has long since ceased, due to bad relations with Turkey. This estrangement from the neighboring continent, bred of hatred and fear, is traumatic, cutting it off from its natural trading area, including the picturesque and productive littoral that once was part of Ionia.

Obviously, things of the spirit, both good and bad, still dominate human affairs. Also, as we know, human affairs either progress or retrogress; they never stand still. The modern West, for instance, adjudged as a law-abiding society, is shockingly primitive in comparison to what it was in Ionian times. Also, nobility, in the best sense of the word, is now in eclipse, to our social impoverishment. Likewise, our sense of curiosity may have atrophied, so that now we are barely acquainted with our cultural homeland, if at all.

Nowadays giant ferryboats from Piraeus, the port of Athens, come to Mytilene twice a week via Chios. On Chios Greece's wealthiest families now maintain summer homes in an exclusive colony. These residential anchors to smart addresses in Athens, London, and New York provide a common playground for their children and a yearly rendezvous for youthful friendships to be renewed and, hopefully, to lead to matrimony. "Chios money," garnered by ships roaming the globe, should not be dissipated on outlanders. That's the local credendum. And the leviathans that call here briefly each week, keeping Chios well supplied with necessities and luxuries, manifest merely a small part of a worldwide maritime wealth. They also demonstrate that big business wastes no time, for very tight schedules are strictly adhered to.

Three blasts from a big ship's deep-throated whistle, echoing from the hills, signal its arrival in Mytilene. The ferryboat backs up to its dock with surprising manageability and drops its steel tailgate, and scores of heavily loaded trucks and trailer-trucks rumble off, making deliveries to insular customers directly from mainland warehouses and factories. Private cars, motorcycles, mopeds, and a confusing surge of hundreds of debarking and boarding passengers add to the dockside bedlam.

This heavily subsidized maritime service, combined with subsidized daily flights by Olympic Airways from Athens, maintains Lesbos as a viable ward of the Greek government. As a result, all local matters, including such trivia as the date for a proposed beauty contest, are now decided in Athens. Obviously, modern democracy has many forms, as it had in Ionian times.

Come evening, though, Mytilene reasserts its individuality. People swarm to the bayfront. Neatly dressed in crisp clothing after the heat of the day, their faces shining, they are out to find joy. They come mostly in family groups, which smilingly pause for mutual greetings and often quickly commingle, with young friends eagerly bombarding each other with the latest juvenile gossip.

The festive mood of the crowded esplanade is matched by a note of nautical gaiety. A flotilla of pleasure yachts moored on the abutting bayfront, their landing gear out and various national flags flying from stern posts, have their riggings festooned with pennants and other colorful bunting as a salute to Mytilene's traditional evening festivities. Across the esplanade, sidewalk cafés overflow with lively chatter, laughter, and wisps of tantalizing perfumes. Waiters hustle, for after a sleepy afternoon, the day's big business has finally begun.

A shout goes up from somewhere in the milling crowd; an accordion starts playing; a space has been cleared for folk dancing. People join in the quick rhythm with alacrity. Not far away, voices erupt in choral song and blend into a swelling harmony. The daily festival is under way. And always there are the young couples walking hand in hand, keeping a little apart from the others, seemingly oblivious of all others, as if they were caught up in a love beyond earthly understanding. That's the stuff that Sappho gloried in and sang of and crucified herself on what, to her, was its single imperfection.

Addendum for Zealots and Budding Scholars

Introduction

The beginnings of Greek history are lost in an irrecoverable past, and though the first decipherable records come from about 1400 B.C., yet the story, as far as we can reconstruct it from the Greeks' own thoughts, begins with the Homeric poems in the last part of the eighth century.

—C. M. Bowra

Writing on the Palace of Minos in the *Monthly Review* for March 1901, Sir Arthur Evans said: "Less than a generation back the origin of Greek civilization, and with it the sources of all great culture that has ever been, were wrapped in an impenetrable mist. That ancient world was still girt round within its narrow confines by the circling 'Stream of Ocean.' Was there anything beyond? The fabled kings and heros of the Homeric Age, with its palaces and strongholds, were they aught, after all, but more or less humanized sun myths?"

A people lives by its geography. What nature provides as a home and background is a most decisive and enduring element in any people's history. The peculiar position of Ionia on Asia's southwest coast, close to the world's earliest civilizations, with cultured and rich neighbors, and inheriting a lively and multifarious mythology, largely determined its destiny. Of course, Ionians themselves deserve credit for discerning the best opportunities and being trustworthy merchants and agents who served their foreign customers well.

157

I: A Quest for Happiness

A quest for personal happiness may be wrong, for it lacks nobility and its ambiance is stultifyingly small. Rather, seek to join a creative community, exhilaratingly free. . . .

. . . it is a secret to be pursued . . . and surely to be found; for out of the most hard and barbarous times, out of strangely modern vicissitudes, sacking of cities, emigration, slavery, exile—it still hangs unmistakably, elusive, like a sea-spray in the sun, over the coastline of Ionia . . .

To catch even the echo a thousand times weakened and repeated of the authentic voice of happiness is worth a journey. To have heard it and not to hand it on, however faintly, would be grudging indeed. I shall try—asking only this of my readers—that they believe in the forgotten rapture. If they doubt, let them read the fragments left us, let them see the smiling faces of the young men and women . . . let them look into the busy lives of those philosophers, running their politics, their poetry, their engineering, their hypotheses between one exile and another. The felicity, the zest and the buoyancy of life is there, and they flourished in danger . . .

How shall I give it a name? Those things have an unreal reality, like mermaids, difficult to hold. They exist, but the uses of language fail . . . the foot as light as thistledown and gone, the robe that is only a silken rustle disappearing, the gleam flashing quicker than sight—evoked through twenty-five centuries of time.

—Freya Stark in *Ionia—a Quest*

II: Hard by the Oldest Battlegrounds of the World, Somebody Is Singing

Great Peace bringeth forth for men wealth and the flower of

honey-tongued songs and for the Gods the yellow flame of the burning of the thighs of oxen and fleecy sheep upon the fine-wrought altars, and for the young a desire for disport of body and for flute and festal dance. Meanwhile in the iron-bound shield throng hang the warps of the brown spider, headed spear and two-edged sword are whelmed in an ever-spreading rust, and the noise of the brazen trumpet is not; nor is reft from our eyelids that honey-hearted sleep which soothes the spirit towards dawn. The streets are abloom with delightful feasting and the hymns of children go up like a flame.

—Bacchylides

III: The Ages of Antiquity

Stone Age:	Paleolithic	(before 8000 B.C.)
	Mesolithic	(8000–7000 B.C.)
	Neolithic	(7000–3000 B.C.)
Bronze Age:		(3000–1100 B.C.)

Troy's earliest city dates from about 3000; the Troy that fell to the Greeks about 1184 was believed to be the seventh city built on the ruins of its predecessors.

Iron Age: (1100 B.C.–present)

Ionia's story takes place in the nascent Iron Age. However, Sappho, like all Ionians, was surrounded by things of bronze, rather than of iron, for the substitution of the stronger metal in domestic utensils, added to the imperious demand for iron weapons of war and harder tools (cutting the fluting of marble, for instance, needed tools of iron), was extremely gradual.

Does it seem strange that both we and the Ionians live in the Iron Age? That's how science classifies us. And it's correct. Timewise, we and our cultural ancestors are like next-door neighbors. Despite intervening centuries, in fact, we're closer to the ancient Greeks than any people since, except modern Europeans.

IV: Sunrise Land in the Nascent Iron Age

The Hittites may have dominated Anatolia throughout the Bronze Age and ushered in the Iron Age. They were pioneer craftsmen in that metal. Their capital, Hattusas, was located near the great bend of the Halys River, the longest in Anatolia. It empties into the Black Sea.

This rolling region of moderately fertile valleys and grassy hills affords a good mixture for pastoral and settled agriculture. The massive walls of Hattusas still stand, a contemporary of Egypt's Temple of Thebes, mutely testifying to the masterful power of the people who mysteriously vanished just before the Trojan War began.

Among the foreign peoples who came into Anatolia and settled there during the Hittite ascendancy, or immediately afterward, were the Phrygians, Lydians, and possibly Carians. They were well established when the first mass migration of Greeks arrived about 1150 B.C., coming by sea, not by land as their predecessors did.

V: Hesiod Speaks

For here is now an age of iron. Never by daytime will there

be an end to hard work and pain, nor in the night to weariness, when the gods will send anxieties to trouble us. Yet here also there shall be some good things mixed with the evils . . .

—from *Works & Days*

VI: The Sea People Arrive, Settle Down, and React to the Fearful Challenges Confronting Them

Homer calls them Achaeans; they call themselves Hellenes and their homeland Hellas. Not until modern times do Englishmen call them Greeks and their country Greece. These second sons and their adventurous companions, leaving home either as surplus progeny or other landless and willful youths, took native wives and built families of their own. Six generations, or about two centuries, may have been required for them to constitute a full-fledged society. They housed themselves in city-states, providing some safety. But their perilous position in Asia, they knew, demanded much more in order to survive.

VII: Why Archaeologists Dig, Papyrologists Rummage, and Scholars Ponder and Speculate

C. M. Bowra of Oxford, decorated by both England and France for his preeminence as a scholar of ancient Greek, explains why academia has spawned a compelling urge to learn more about ancient Greece:

Our main source of information, the written word, is woefully incomplete. We lack the main part of what was once a rich store of lyric poetry, of early philosophy and history, of early epic except Homer, of many tragedies and comedies. We have hardly a tenth of what the three great Attic tragedians actually wrote, and though the rubbish heaps of Egypt have in recent years yielded precious fragments of lost works, they are only fragments, and make us all the more conscious that Greek literature must have been richer and more various than its surviving remains indicate. The relics of the visual arts are even more tantalizing. In the unequal battle against the depredations of time and the barbarity of man they have survived almost by accident. We have no full-size painting of the classical age; no statues in gold and ivory such as once were the glory of Phidias. Of the many temples which once existed only a few survive, and these are roofless and ruined, robbed long ago of their furniture and treasures. Modern discovery has indeed added much to our knowledge and enlarged our vision, . . . but even the fragments exert so powerful an attraction and have so abundant a vitality that they force us to ask what experience went to their making.

VIII: The Mystery Unfolds

The excitement about Ionia is that here it is no miracle, but the result of causes natural enough if one is patient to hunt for them among the shallows and shiftings of a past that can never be clearly known . . . Commerce and uncertainty together make an adventurous pair, and the coastal cities experienced them to the full. Commerce gave well-being and leisure: there is no poverty about the philosophers of Ionia.

—Freya Stark

IX: A Restless Landmass, and Ambitious Monarchs Are a Constant Threat

Asia's great landmass, restless with the ambitious monarchs of mighty kingdoms, exerted a powerful magnetism as well as an obvious threat. When Assyria brought all the Near East under its sway, commerce accelerated, the tempo of life quickened, and Ionia, sensing *opportunity* as well as increased danger, strengthened its commercial ties with Assyria and more vigorously promoted other arts of peace, such as supplying expert artisans to create monuments and public buildings to glorify victorious monarchs.

There can be no doubt that this current of foreign contacts was of outstanding importance in the development of the Greek people. It gave them an enormous stimulus. This is most tangible in the representational arts.

The sculpture which flourished in the kingdom of Assyria portrayed the deeds of their kings and armies, hunting-scenes and battles, the capture of cities and triumphs in lengthy friezes. The Greeks took from the Assyrians their portrayal of the human form, their style and technique, as they learned them through the mediation of the Syrians, the Phoenicians and the peoples of Asia Minor, but they chose themes from what they regarded as their own history, from the heroic sagas, the songs about the Trojan War and the wanderings of Odysseus, about Heracles' mighty Labors against monsters and giants. Fabulous Greek creatures such as Centaurs rush forward swinging huge trees . . . Art on a large scale, architecture, sculpture, painting, did not become primarily, as it was in the East, a means of glorifying rulers; it was on the contrary entirely at the service of the gods . . . the finest architectural works were the temples of the gods . . . the artistic character of the age can be described as that of a period of searching . . . the achievement of the Greeks remained of lasting value for the whole art of Europe.
—from *Greek and Roman Art,*
by Ernst Ujellberg and Gosta Saglung

Ernst Ujellberg was director of the National Museum in Stockholm and lecturer at Stockholm University.

X: Ionia's Location, Culturally Strategic, Is Climatically Blest

The Ionians chance to have their cities established in the fairest place for climate of all men that we know. For neither the parts to the north nor the parts to the south are like Ionia; for those are oppressed by the cold and the wet, and these by the heat and the drought.

—Herodotus

XI: Assyrian Kings Exploit the Arts of War—Ionians Exploit the Arts of Peace

Believing useful knowledge to be their best defense, Ionians strive to extend that knowledge, like Assyrian kings fought for more territory and worldly riches; thus they begin building the spiritual edifice, later called Hellenism, that molds Western man.

Arnold Toynbee speaks:

From beginning to end, one of the principal seats of the Hellenic civilization was the west coast of Asia Minor which lies, not in Greece, but in Turkey. On the other hand, the northern part of continental European Greece was not fully incorporated in the Hellenic world until the fourth century B.C.

In the last chapter the Romans not only gave political unity and internal peace to all Hellenes around the shores of the Mediterranean by bringing them under a single government; they also gave the Hellenic civilization a second linguistic vehicle, to supplement the Greek language. The official parity of the Greek and Latin languages was justified by the achievement of Cicero, Virgil, Horace, and other great Roman men of letters who produced, in Latin, Hellenic works of art that could bear comparison with the best of those written in Greek.

In this imperial age of Hellenic history, the leading spirits of the Hellenic world were bilingual . . .

XII: That of Which We Are Most Proud Must Justify Our Pride

For he that would live completely happy, must before all things belong to a country that is of good report.

—Simonides

XIII: Ah, Summertime!

The star is coming round again, the season is hard to bear with the world athirst because of the heat; the cricket sounds sweetly from the leaves of the treetop, and lo! the artichoke is blowing.

—Alcaeus

XIV: Let's Relax at an Ionian Banquet in the Sixth Century B.C.

At feasts the guests often drank the common mixture of water and wine to the accompaniment of music. It was held that the music of the lyre and the harp would add to all kinds of pleasure, and prevent drunkenness and gluttony . . . If anyone at any time felt himself losing his temper he would take up his lyre and play to calm his feelings.

Not only . . . was music supposed to sharpen and improve the intellect, soften the dispostion and dissipate sadness, but it was believed that it had even the power to heal disease. Music was a method of mental and moral instruction, and helped to form character. It was not a luxury, but a necessity. It did not develop passion, but controlled it.

—Mary Patrick Mills,
in her *Sappho and the Island of Lesbos*

XV: The Beat Counts Most, Then the Perfume of Words

Alcaeus, also a Lesbian, invented the alcaic strophe, and Sappho perfected the sapphic strophe, . . . achievements which, did not a word of theirs remain, should make them immortal in the annals of poetry and its associated arts of music and dance.

Sappho also wrote in the alcaic, dactylic, glyconic, choriambic, ionic (a minore), and various other metres . . .

More important to the art of poetry, however, was Sappho's invention of "beautiful phrases," which have become an inheritance of the race.

—Symonds

XVI: Wine Is an Indispensable Part of Social Ritual

Wine is poured into water, never vice versa, and the proportion is usually one to three. Ionians are proud of their pure water and can often identify the well from which it comes, as some Turks can today. Also, of course, Ionians are immensely proud of their wine, usually claiming it the world's best.

'Twas a Lydian hand, Asian born, that invented pitchers, and the offerings of toasts in turn round the board with the naming beforehand of the toast to be drunk.

—Critias

And the serving maid, holding the jar aloft, poured out the honey-sweet, mixed one in three.

—Anacreon

XVII: And Music Is a Part of Everything

At banquets, scholia are the high point of the evening. They might be elegant, timely, and witty, but in any case amusing. All guests are expected to participate. When dessert is served, wineglasses refilled, and a jovial mood shared by all, the impromptu songs begin. And despite the good-natured reception accorded each singer, who plays his own accompaniment, it is soon apparent that a good voice, musical talent, and a ready wit are social assets. The host or hostess, of course, knows how to steer things into merriment and laughter.

. . . Symbolic too are the dephnephorica or laurel-bearing songs adopted by the Mytilenians and Simonides and Pindar—written for processions led by a handsome boy, the chosen priest of the year, followed by maidens who carry the pungent branches. These maiden songs with the scent of their hillsides still about them and the pleasant freedom of women, are common to Aeolian, Ionian and Dorian . . .

Not feast days only, but every pattern of daily life was shaped with its appropriate ritual and song—the pipe notes fit for herds of cows and oxen, or what agreed with the goats, what was pleasing to flocks of sheep . . . ; the dance of the wine press, the cutting and gathering . . . carrying of the baskets, then the treading . . . in the press, the turning of the wine into the butts . . . There were the mill songs and the weavers' songs, and one for women winnowing, and lullabies and songs of wailing; and at Athens they used to sing the laws of Charondas.

—Freya Stark, in *Ionia—a Quest*

And, of course, soldiers march to martial music, marriages and joyful paeans go together, and mournful dirges

167

mark life's end. Betweentimes, people hum their favorite ditties.

XVIII: Music, Dancing, Laughter, and the Brotherhood of Scholars

When the day's work is done, whole communities congregate on the main street or square for the happy hours. This means music and dancing, a daily event that may have helped Pythagoras, a brilliant mathematician, to discover that the harmonic intervals of the octave have a numerical ratio. Eventually, the mandatory curriculum that he devised for his Brotherhood of Scholars, geometry, arithmetic, astronomy, and music, was simple but exhaustive. To Pythagoreans, the universe is a living organism and music is the sound of its breathing.

XIX: Choral Singing and Dancing Are Tops, but You Can't Sing with a Foot in Your Mouth

The highest form of music, Greeks believe, is choral singing. This allows full exploitation of the emotional range and also philosophical depth and structural complexity. The chorus is not immobile. The dance in its highest development is woven into one art with choral singing; in fact, they grew up together. The word *foot*, as meaning part of a verse, owes its origins to the dance that accompanied the song. Also, as Will Durant points out, in the life of Greece *orchestra* originally meant a dancing platform, usually in front of the stage.

XX: Does Everybody Dance?

Well, not quite everybody. Unborn babes and people in their coffins are excluded, although about the latter, gossip says, there is some doubt. In any case, dancing alone is customary; so is dancing by couples and dancing in groups, particularly groups. Folk dancing must be carried on in heaven, for how else can Greeks be happy?

XXI: The Body Speaks, Whispers, and Humbly Adores

So the chorus dances. Its body language supplements the voice to express joy, sorrow, ecstasy, agony, wrath—all the raging emotions and grand passions, as well as the infinite gradations of mood that human beings feel. The dance is often a supplication to the gods, full of reverence and humility, like a communal prayer.

XXII: Athens Salutes Ionia

And he who once wove poems for women's songs, Anacreon, whom Teos gave to Greece, the stimulator of banquets, the deceiver of women, the antagonist of flutes, lover of the lyre, sweet, free from pain. Never shall love of thee grow old or die, as long as the boy serves the water mixed with wine, from left to right, and female choirs ply the dance all night long, and the bowl, the daughter of bronze . . . [holds] the drops of Dionysus.

—Critias of Athens

XXIII: Even an Ionian Poet, Lover of Wine and All the Rites of Love, Sappho's Coeval, Has Sobering Thoughts

Betwixt thee and me let there be truth, the most righteous of all things.

—Mimnermus of Colophon

XXIV: Feminism Blooms, Then Disappears for More than Two Thousand Years

The customs of the Aeolians permitted more social and domestic freedom than was common in Greece. Aeolian women were not confined . . . or subjected to the rigorous discipline of the Spartans. While mixing freely with the male society, they were highly educated, and accustomed to express their sentiments to an extent unknown elsewhere in history—until indeed, the present time. The Lesbian ladies applied themselves successfully to literature. They formed clubs for the cultivation of poetry and music. They studied the arts of beauty, and sought to refine metrical forms and diction. Nor did they confine themselves to the scientific side of art. Unrestrained by public opinion, and passionate for the beautiful, they cultivated their senses and emotions . . .

—Symonds

In short, all the obvious factors, and others beyond our ken, were there to bring about full female participation in society. One aspect thereof was the popularity of the contests in the arts (painting, poetry, architecture, etc.), whether Panionian, Olympic, or local intercity. They caused more excitement, particularly choral singing and the dance, than athletic contests. The former didn't survive, it seems, even in "the glorious fifth century B.C.," when feminism lost its bloom. In that century, the three great tragedians dominated the performing arts.

XXV: What Is Good Can Also Be Evil

Gold is the child of Zeus; neither moth nor worm devours it, and it overpowers the strongest of mortal minds.

—Sappho

Here again, temperance seems indispensable to righteousness, and Sappho was its practitioner, despite allegations of her extremism.

XXVI: The Ionian Alphabet

The Greek alphabet occupies in many ways a unique place in the history of writing. Although the Greeks did not invent the alphabet, they improved it to such a degree that for 3,000 years it has furnished the most convenient vehicle of communication and expression for the thoughts of many peoples, creeds and tongues. They also gave the alphabet symmetry of art. There were several local Greek alphabets, but they gradually moved in the direction of uniformity. In 403 B.C. the Ionic alphabet of Miletus was officially adopted at Athens, and in the following half century this action was followed by the other mainland states as well.

—Cambridge History of Christianity

The date when the Phoenician alphabet was taken up by the ancient Greeks and spread through their city-states has been put from before 1,000 B.C. to as late as 700 B.C. The oldest inscriptions date from the eighth century B.C., but the Greek alphabet, occupying a supreme position in the evolution of graphic communication, may have developed earlier. The Greeks took the Phoenician or northern Semitic alphabet and changed five consonants to make words. These have evolved into *a, e, i, o, u* . . . Local Greek areas adopted the alphabet to their own needs, then two versions—the Chalcidian in the west and the Ionic in the east—became dominant. Near the end of the fifth century B.C., Athens officially adopted the Ionic version which became standard throughout Greece.

—Robert B. Meggs,
A History of Graphic Design

XXVII: Words Come First, for Men Must Communicate. Ionia, the Kingdom of Words, Is a Linguistic Gold Mine. Where to Start? With Homer? Hesiod? Or the Dancing Words of Sappho?

Never before . . . and never since, did the human soul, in the grip of a fiery passion, utter a cry like hers; and . . . in directness, in lucidity, in that high imperious verbal economy which only nature can teach the artist, she has no equal, and none worthy to take the place of second.

—Theodore Watts-Dunton

Still like sparkles of Greek fire,
Burn on through time and ne'er expire.

—Thomas Moore on fragments
of Sappho's verse

Strabo, writing in the Augustan Age, challenged all history to find a poetess approaching Sappho "in the slightest degree," an opinion echoed by *The Encyclopedia Britannica* (9th ed.), which avers she is "incomparably the greatest poetess the world has ever seen." Swinburne called her "the greatest poet who ever lived."

172

The world has suffered no greater literary loss than the loss of Sappho's poems. So perfect are the smallest fragments preserved . . . that we muse in a sad rapture of astonishment to think what the complete poems must have been . . . Among the ancients Sappho enjoyed a unique renown . . . Nowhere is a hint whispered that her poetry was aught but perfect. As far as we can judge, these praises were strictly just. Of all the poets of the world, of all the illustrious artists of all literatures, Sappho is one whose every word has a peculiar and unmistakable perfume, a seal of absolute perfection and inimitable grace.

—Symonds

XXVIII: Education? The World's Best. And It Never Stopped.

To begin with, parents taught their young children, and assigned their most intelligent slave exclusively to that task. And the apprentice system prevailed in such trades as winemaking, textiles, furniture, ceramics, etc. In the arts and athletics, the masters were supposed to teach all qualified beginners. Indeed, all capable adults taught classes as needed, and often attended other classes themselves. In short, education was the fashion. And also a patriotic duty.

Of course, all males continued military training until old age. Ionia's School of Philosophy broke new ground. And the medical school also. And Sappho's finishing school for girls, and rival institutions, proved that education was not a state monopoly. Freedom reigned. Nevertheless, the whole city-state resembled a school. Games and contests, intercity, regional, topped by the Olympics, were something to strive for. Prizes won belonged to the city-state, not the individual.

XXIX: Mytilene's Illustrious Neighbors

To the south was Chios, Homer's isle, and across the channel on the mainland was Cyme, the busy port where Hesiod was born. Nearby was Phocaea, "a city of moderate size, skilled in nothing but to rear great men," according to Diogenes Laertius.

The Phocaeans, fiercely loving freedom, totally abandoned their city when Harpagus drew close. (Harpagus, a Mede, was the Persians' best general.) Abroad, Phocaeans founded several well-known cities, including Nice and Marseilles.

XXX: Semper Fidelis

"The women of Chios were noted for their beauty," Plutarch says, "but there has not been a case for adultery brought before its courts for 700 years." Is fidelity the backbone of a noble life-style?

XXXI: "Art Is Long, Life Is Short . . ."

Scarcely any feature of Greek art is more impressive to the student than its continuous and uninterrupted course. When once it has started it does not turn back, but goes forward steadily, for a time rising superior to difficulty after difficulty, attaining a higher and higher level, then in the fifth century branching out in various directions into styles and groups, then going on with great technical skill, but with a loss of inspiration. It has a course of evolution as steady as that of any kind of plant or animal. This shows that it did not depend upon the rise of successive men of talent or genius, each of

174

whom was intent upon expressing himself; but upon the rise and influence of successive artistic schools, each of which did not merely follow the personality of a founder or teacher, but stood for a phase in the development of the common life of the Greek people. The schools were Ionian or Dorian, Attic or Argive, and harmonized with the whole civilization of such fractions of the race. Ionian art went with the gay and plea-sure-loving ways of the Asiatic coast. Dorian art reflected the restraint, the balance, the self-control of the people of the Peloponnesus. Attic art not only conformed to the refined taste of the people of Athens, but suited also the strong mental bias of the most intellectual city which ever existed. Of course, these schools did not flourish in complete isolation one from the other; city influenced city and artist artist; but in a far less degree than would be the case now. A school of sculpture was a species; and all the individuals of a species were more like one another than they were like any of their contemporar-ies outside . . . Greece was pre-eminently the land of produc-tive guilds, of families of artists, of groups of workers who were of one heart and one spirit, and who therefore worked in one style . . . Severally in all great periods of art there is such fellowship . . . They must have had what we should call a collective personality. It is more than probable that among the workers on the Parthenon were Alcamenes and Agoracri-tus, two sculptors who rose to great fame. It was certain that among the workers on the Erechtheum was Praxias, a pupil of Calamis, and probably a relative of Praxiteles. The distinction between artist and mason, so marked in our day, scarcely existed in Greece. The mason who had talent became a noted sculptor; and the sculptor, instead of making a model in wax or plaster, set to work, like Michelangelo, on the block of marble himself. Probably sometimes, like Benvenuto Cellini, he cast his own bronze statues.

—Percy Gardner, F.B.A.

Merton Professor of Classical Archaeology

at the University of Oxford

XXXII: Painting, the Most Perishable Art

The later part of the fourth century B.C. was regarded by critics as the golden age of painting. The name of Apelles always shone brightest in the artistic firmament and it was not even overshadowed by the names of the greatest sculptors. By the side of Apelles were many other painters of distinction. Protogenes, Action, Antiphilos and others. The ancient paintings preserved from the cities devastated by Vesuvius in 79 A.D. lend support to the impressions to be derived from literature. The paintings found there are largely copies and derivations of Greek originals from the latter part of the fourth century and the early Hellenistic period, the classic period of ancient painting.

—Kjellberg

"Apelles of Cos," says Pliny the Elder, "surpassed all the other painters who either preceded or succeeded him. Single-handed, he contributed more to painting than all the others together . . . A picture by Apelles sold for a sum equal to the treasures of whole cities."

Born on Kos, Apelles spent most of his productive years in Ephesus.

XXXIII: Art, Properly Perceived, Teaches Us Humility

If once the idea of beauty as an end to be aimed at be expelled from art, art sinks like a stone to the bottom of the sea. Some people are ready to tolerate any monstrosity in art, however remote from nature, however offensive to decency, however repugnant to humanity. The whole artistic inheritance of the race from the day when man first began to climb out of barbarism is liable to be thrown away by an age which has unbounded confidence in its own wisdom.

—Sir Gilbert Murray

XXXIV: The Greeks Infuse Stone with Life

Egyptians were the teachers of the Greek sculptor in the execution of the standing naked male figure, which was to play so important a role in Greek sculpture. The static unchanging element in the Egyptian portrayal of the male, which is the direct result of the special conditions of Egyptian art, did not suit the Greek character. In Greece, too, sculptors served a religious purpose, but its ideal foundation was the athletically perfect male body. In Egyptian sculpture the human figure had lost all trace of the unrest which is part and parcel of life on this side of the grave—the Greek "Kouro" from its very beginning are full of restrained dynamic force and embody the brilliant possibilities of human existence.

—Kjellberg

XXXV: Architecture

The pinnacle of architectural achievement in the West remains the Acropolis at Athens, created in the fifth century B.C. That was architecture's Golden Age. The Silver Age, following in the wake of Alexander's conquests, demonstrates that architecture, and indeed all art, does not necessarily reflect an inflated ego, nor an abundance of wealth or power; art, in all of its impulses and final forms, is forever elusive, coy, and manufactured by an individual, or group of individuals, in ways that even they cannot explain.

The three orders of Greek architecture are the Dorian, Ionian, and Corinthian. The latter did not appear until the fourth century B.C., and it is comparatively ornate and vulgar, reaching full bloom under the Romans. The Dorian was the mainstay of Greek architecture. Either fluted or plain, it was stout, strong, utilitarian. The Ionian probably appeared first, the fond handiwork of Asian Greeks who had long known the pillars that upheld temples in Egypt and Babylon. It was slim, elegant, and seemingly delicate, yet strong enough to uphold beauty and be an integral part of a singular harmony.

The Greeks had discovered that the post and the lintel comprised the only basics of the structure they needed. They were primarily interested in constructing temples to their gods, employing all their ingenuity and inspiration to make them worthy, and therefore beautiful. They also constructed town halls, marketplaces, covered walks for shade, odeums, gymnasiums, theaters, and private homes for citizens, combining utility and attractiveness, but these were of secondary importance; they belonged to the body of life, its physical side, whereas temples belonged to its spiritual side, which brought life to everything.

The Romans were more inventive builders. They inherited Greek culture, but not its intensity, and were therefore inferior artisans and artists. Seeking to reach beyond the limitation of the post and lintel, wanting more unobstructed space, they arrived at the arch, the vault, and the dome. They became the world's greatest builders.

XXXVI: Is Art the Best Guide to History, As Some Scholars Say?

History books are almost totally concerned with politics—emperors, kings, presidents, governments, and wars. Little is said about the people, their daily life, their thoughts and aspirations. Artists may be paid to glorify rulers, but great artists also reflect the life of the people, their principal activities and the moods of the time, and they do so with revealing empathy and sensitivity. Consider this observation by Kjellberg:

Within the Greek cities themselves a great ferment was taking place. The old aristocracy had been shaken by the economic development which introduced trade and industrial activity—important levers for the growth and prosperity of society. The warrior charioteers of the aristocracy, who fought with spears in single combat, had to give place to the citizen hoplite army which advanced in tightly-closed lines.

Great sculptors have left us excellent models of each, as well as other visual confirmations of a changing society.

XXXVII: Not the First, Just the Best

Before the birth of Greek art, fully developed civilizations had indeed existed for thousands of years in Mesopotamia, Egypt, and Crete; but from its earliest appearance Greek art quickly rose to dominate the entire Mediterranean areas. Its underlying principles—which we call "classical"—imposed themselves over the whole of the ancient world. While other civilizations, reaching the end of their development, became exhausted, classical art . . . spread through the provinces of Alexander's great empire, gave form to the art of Imperial Rome, and remained the vital inheritance and basic premise for all European art.

> —Giovanni Becatti,
> in *The Art of Ancient Greece and Rome*

XXXVIII: Mathematics and Astronomy

The beginnings of trigonometry may go back to Archimedes (*Measurements of a Circle*), but Hipparchus was the first person who can be proved to have used trigonometry systematically. Hipparchus, the greatest astronomer of antiquity, whose observations were made between 161 and 126 B.C., discovered the precession of the equinoxes, calculated the mean lunar month at 29 days, 12 hours, 44 minutes, 2.5 seconds (an error of less than a second from the presently accepted figure), made more correct estimates of the sizes and distances of the sun and moon than existed previously, introduced great improvements in the instruments used for observations, and compiled a catalog of some 850 stars, their position stated in terms of latitude and longitude (in relation to the ecliptic). He wrote a treatise in *Twelve Books on Chords in a Circle* equivalent to a table of trigonometrical sines. For calculating areas in astronomy from other arcs given by means of tables he used propositions in spherical trigonometry.

XXXIX: Medicine

The body beautiful needs care, and the Greeks strive to provide it.

To realize the nature of our medical system, some knowledge of its Greek sources is essential. It would indeed be a bad day for medicine if ever this debt to the Greeks were forgotten, and the loss would be at least as much ethical as intellectual . . . The texts of Hippocrates and Galen have now ceased to occupy a place in any medical curriculum. Yet all who know these writings, know too, not only that their spirit is still with us, but that the works themselves form the background of modern practice, and that their very phraseology is still in use at the bedside. Modern medicine may be truly described as in essence a creation of the Greeks.

—Charles Singer,
in *The Legacy of Greece*

XL: Religion, First Phase

The universe is a manifestation of divinity, the Greeks believed. And because their environment was something alive, they invested all aspects of it, such as mountains, brooks, or trees, with their own gods or goddesses. The sun, mighty Apollo, was sovereign by day, and at night the sky was a dazzling spectacle of moon, stars, constellations, planets, and other heavenly bodies, all of which had their own divinity and exerted their superior power upon the earth.

Men envied the gods, for they possessed eternal youth, free of worldly cares and tribulations. Man strove to be more like the gods. And the acropolis, or high city, was reserved for divinities; there men built beautiful temples to them. Every day, however, whether in city or field or at sea, men consorted with the gods, for they were part of nature. Religion, to the Greeks, was something very intimate. It was the invisible blood of their lives. In comparison, Christianity is intimately woven into the everyday lives of comparatively few people.

XLI: The Ultimate Loneliness

Subtly, in every day, they find the immortal pulse, making a sacrament of life, whatever the god may be; and this image of the eternal in his existence is what the exile loses, because the familiar unconscious ways to find it have been broken, unless he can build something more safely permanent in his own heart. The break is not irreparable, but generations are needed to build a new tradition in a different shape.

—Freya Stark

Athenian colonists on Lemnos commissioned Phidias, the greatest sculptor of that time, to make them a statue of

Athena, and this Lemnian Athena was considered by many critics to be his most beautiful work. For the Greeks on Lemnos, at least, she banished the ultimate loneliness and brought them home to their religion, to comfort, to spiritual security.

XLII: Literature's Grand Congress of Words

The Greeks are justly admired for individual poems, plays, and pieces of writing; but it was something even greater to have explored the possibilities of literature so far that posterity, while it has developed Greek genres, has not hitherto been able to add to them. This is one part of the Greek legacy to literature.

—R. W. Livingston,
in *The Legacy of Greece*

Though one of the Greek tragedians may seem rather greater and more complete than another, their work as a whole has a single pervading quality. It is marked by grandeur, excellence, sanity, complete humanity, a high philosophy of life, a lofty way of thinking, a powerful intuition. We find these qualities in their surviving lyric and epic poetry as well as in their drama: we find them in their philosophers, orators, and historians and, to an equally high degree, in their surviving sculpture . . . Besides the great Attic poets, like Aeschylus and Sophocles, I am absolutely nothing.

—Goethe, in *Gesprache*

The period which intervened between the birth of Pericles and the death of Aristotle is undoubtedly, whether considered in itself or with reference to the effects which it has produced upon the subsequent destinies of civilized man, the most memorable in the history of the world . . . The wrecks and fragments of the subtle and profound minds, like the ruins of a fine statue, obscurely suggest to us the grandeur and perfection of the whole. Their very language . . . in variety, in simplicity, in flexibility, and in copiousness, exceeds every other language of the western world.

—Shelley,
in "On the Manners of the Ancients"

XLIII: The Italian Renaissance and the Greek Renaissance Were Cultural Volcanos to Greatness

The history of the world consists mostly in the memory of those ages, quite few in number, in which some part of the world has risen above itself and burst into flower or fruit . . . For most races and nations during most of their life are not progressive but simply stagnant, sometimes just managing to preserve their standard customs, sometimes slipping back to the slough.

The rare periods, the creative periods, are easy enough to recognize, for there will be exhilaration in the air, a sense of walking on new paths, of dawning hopes and untried possibilities, a confidence that all things can be one if only we try hard enough. In that sense the world will be young . . . And it is that youth which is half the secret of the Greek spirit.

—Sir Gilbert Murray

XLIV: School Days May Be Forever

Cities are the teachers of men

—Simonides

XLV: My, but You Smell Sweet

Have you seen the new flasks in human and animal forms? They're containers for all sorts of perfumes and scented oils. The best ones, they say, come from Rhodes, where attar of roses is made. Ten thousand roses or more are needed to make a single ounce of that volatile oil, which makes only a dollop of perfume.

Cosmetics, expensive perfumes, and all kinds of beauty aids were a fragmented industry before Sappho's time, when feminism came into bloom. The latter, however, probably gave the beauty business a tremendous boost, demanding better quality, something different and new, and the exclusive use, say, of a rare perfume—like the Caesars restricted the color purple to royalty.

XLVI: Astrology, Older than Astronomy, Is Still Kicking

Greek philosophers struggled hard and long to liberate nascent astronomy from the superstitions of astrology. The latter, native to both Egypt and Chaldea (ancient Babylonia), was initially their own religion, spawning all others. Monarchs relied on what the stars foretold about the future to guide their actions. Wars wouldn't be started, for instance, if heavenly signs weren't propitious. Astrologers had tremendous power. The priest who read the stars could assure the pharaoh and the public, for instance, that the Nile would flood again this year at the regular time, and they were venerated. Whereas astrology in the East was concerned exclusively with happenings of royal or public import, the Greeks democratized it. The heavenly bodies, led by the sun by day and by the moon, stars, planets, and constellations at night,

184

obviously ruled the earth and everybody upon it. In the Greek view, each person had a horoscope. The aspect of stars at his birth, including the signs of the Zodiac, and their relative positions and aspects thereafter govern his life. He will have lucky days, ordinary days, and bad days. A good astrologer can foretell them, or so people believed. As a result, astrology made phenomenal progress in Greece. Soon, priests, soothsayers, and other practitioners of the occult science in the East were coming there to study, reversing the former trend. One Berosus, priest of Baal, for instance, established himself on Kos about 280 B.C., to learn the "sacred chorus of the skies." On Kos, astrology and medicine commingled under the priests of Aesculapius and were never entirely separated, despite the successes of Hippocrates. On Kos, too, no doubt, astrology had its converts among the Ptolemies, and one can envision the young Arsinoes, Berenices, and Cleopatras excitedly discussing their horoscopes. Juvenal reports a pampered Roman lady who wouldn't move without consulting her astrologer, whether to receive a lover, go to market, or ask a favor of the emperor. But perhaps the most typical believer in astrology was Tiberius.

Tiberius, the emperor when Christ was crucified, had retired as the army's first general to study astrology on Rhodes. They were the happiest years of his life. He met daily with scholars in a shady garden to discuss the mystical language of the stars—a spectacle he had watched in military camps for about four decades. Rhodes, where Julius Caesar had also studied, was still considered Rome's "schoolhouse." However, Tiberius's student days were cut short by a summons from Augustus; the first emperor, to whom Tiberius was related by marriage, had adopted him as a son. He was to return to Rome immediately. He was to be groomed for the world's highest office.

Like Augustus, Tiberius was a stern moralist. After he put on the purple and ruled as a royal loner, it is doubtful if he would have survived the many troubles that overwhelmed him if, before retiring for the night, he didn't draw strength and renewed hope from his lonely vigils of star gazing.

Today, few major cities are without newspapers that carry daily horoscopes. And astrology has gained important ancillary phenomena. For a while, our skies were full of flying saucers. Then spaceships appeared. A whole literature grew up about other inhabited planets. Some scientists seriously assert that many planets are similar to ours, so life thereon, resembling *Homo sapiens*, is not unlikely. The people who believe this far-out speculation have, in that respect, an outlook like that of Emperor Tiberius and the many Greeks and Romans like him. They would feel at home together.

XLVII: Let's Relax Again in the Sixth Century B.C.

This is the sort of thing we should say by the fireside in the wintertime, after we lie on soft couches after a good meal drinking sweet wine and crunching chick-peas: "Of what country are you, good sir? And how old were you when the Mede appeared?"

—Xenophanes

XLVIII: The Medes and the Persians

These two non-Semitic peoples (neither Arabs nor Jews and related to each other as Aryans) occupied the Median Empire in the eastern uplands. After Cyrus-the-Great conquered his neighboring tribes, however, the Median Empire became known as the Persian Empire, and much feared.

When Cyrus overran Nineveh, bringing down Assyrian power in 550 B.C., he dominated the Near East.

The Persian Empire extended from the Halys River in Anatolia to Kabul, capital of present-day Afghanistan. The Medes and the Persians continued to fight as one people under the dynasty of great Persian kings—Cyrus, Darius, and Xerxes. They extended their overlordship to Egypt and Europe, conquering the Scythians on Russia's southern steppes and almost conquering mainland Greece.

Their first strategic conquest was Lydia. They did not try to subdue the Ionians, who were useful to them and whom they admired. Also, Lydia was an adequate military springboard to the West.

The Persians divided their empire into almost twenty provinces, each ruled by a satrap. Sardis was the main satrapy in the West. The empire's backbone was the sixteen-hundred-mile Royal Road from Sardis to Susa, the Persian capital near the Persian Gulf. Inns—perhaps the world's first hotels—provided lodgings for Persian nobility traveling in litters. The ordinary journey from Susa to Sardis took about three months. Mail was carried in five days by a relay of riders on fresh horses.

Because Susa was sweltering in summer, Cyrus started building another capital, Parsa, in the mountains. Cyrus's two successors completed the grandiose capital, which combined elegance, luxury, and beauty with its lofty solitude. The Greeks called it Persepolis, and that name stuck like the name Persia itself. Indeed, Greek stonemasons, architects, and sculptors toiled there, some of them for most of their lives, to make Persepolis a civic masterpiece. Deserted now, it is still the crowning human achievement in all of Persia, including Iran's modern works.

XLIX: What Became of Croesus?

The richest man in the world was frightened when the Persians began absorbing the Medes. That meant that a powerful coalition of warlike peoples was forming on his border. What to do? Croesus, who also aspired to be a military conqueror, decided to strike first, before the Medes and Persians were fully united. He won. Cyrus suddenly withdrew from the battlefield. Croesus returned home triumphantly. Shortly thereafter, when winter set in and armies were traditionally demobilized, Cyrus invaded Lydia. The surprised Lydians were easily defeated, and Croesus was taken captive. Legend says that when Solon, the great Athenian statesman, had visited Sardis previously, Croesus had told him that he also wanted to be known as the world's happiest man. No man could be so judged until after his death, Solon had replied. But about Croesus's death there are only rumors. Some people say he expired on a flaming funeral pyre with his wives, confined there by his conqueror; some say he became an ornament in the King of Kings' court in Susa; some say he merely faded into oblivion.

Well, not quite oblivion. His memory lingers on. And the oral tradition winnowed out the bad as superfluous trivia. Long after the fall of Sardis, Pindar wrote: "The loving kindness of Croesus fadeth not away."

L: The Father of History Speaks

Herodotus (c. 480–429 B.C.), born in Halicarnassus, was a bon vivant. He enjoyed life. And he tried to savor all of life's delectations. In short, he was typically Ionian. On the serious side, he set himself the gargantuan task of writing *The*

History of the Persian Wars. Otherwise, Herodotus feared that unforgettable conflict that recently shook the world would become too blurred in memory.

Herodotus traveled far and wide and in his later years settled in Athens, where he made his living by reciting his history. These writings covered many peoples and lands in addition to Greeks and Persians. They were composed, in no small part, as good stories, which would captivate and hold an audience's attention. Most of his facts are undoubtedly true, and his fictions, in all probability, also faithfully reflect the temper of the time and the characters involved. And although we should heed Hecateus, an illustrious predecessor, who says in a surviving fragment: "Beware of the stories of the Greeks, for they are ridiculous," we can accept Herodotus's stories when they are supported by common sense and other known facts. In any case, we have no other history of antiquity.

Herodotus spoke highly of the Persians. He praised their training of young boys in good horsemanship, how to shoot arrows straight, and to speak the truth. Their government functioned efficiently. Cyrus, Darius, and Xerxes were able monarchs who, ruling by divine right, commanded the fealty of their nobles, each of whom had been given a great fief and was left pretty much alone as long as he delivered his allotment of taxes and military levies.

Darius assembled the empire's might to strike at mainland Greece in 490 B.C., but he was turned back at Marathon and Thermopylae, sending those names ringing down through the ages. Xerxes struck again ten years later, almost totally destroying Athens, but the Greeks defeated his navy at Salamis and followed that decisive victory with a land victory at Plataea, forcing the Persians to retreat and never to cross the Hellespont again into Europe.

These two momentous victories inaugurated "the glorious fifth century B.C." Pericles, born three years before Salamis, the scion of an aristocratic family that had served Athens courageously and well, was subsequently elected to the highest Athenian office for thirty years. He demonstrated, some say, that democracy achieves its best results when its vigor and variety are skillfully directed by a strong-willed aristocrat of unassailable probity and impeccable cultural taste.

LI: Stories May Be Untrue Yet Tell the Truth

Herodotus reports:

Croesus purposed to build ships and lay hands on the people of the isles. But when he had all things ready . . . there came to Sardis, as some say, Bias of Priene, but others say, Pittacus of Mytilene, and prevented the building of ships, for when Croesus asked him if there was any new thing in Greece, he said: "O King, the people of the isles are buying ten thousand horses, having in mind to make war against thee in Sardis." And Croesus, believing what he spoke true, said: "O that the Gods might put this thing into the hearts of the people of the isles, to come against the children of Lydia on horseback." And he answered and said: "O King . . . thou dost earnestly pray to catch the people of the isles on land riding horses . . . But what else deemest thou that the people of the isles pray for . . . than to catch the Lydians at sea." Then Croesus ceased from the building of ships, and covenanted friendship with the Ionians that dwell in the isles.

LII: What's a Pelisse?

If you don't know what a pelisse is, that shows you've never been to Sardis.

—Aristophanes

Sardis had the same fascination in antiquity that Paris had in nineteenth-century Europe. For the rich and famous, it was the "in" place, the place to be seen. Big shots in the clothing trade, the jewelry trade, or anything dependent on fashion went there regularly. Bankers and statesmen were also attracted to the city because of its preeminence in matters of money and finance.

LIII: An Imperial View from Chios

Ionia's offshore islands—Lesbos, Chios, Samos, Kos, and Rhodes—are not unlike box seats at the opera. They have a commanding view of the stage yet still guard the observers' insular privacy. Let us heed, then, this offshore view of Freya Stark, seeing clearly with loving eyes:

Of all the nations of Asia, the Persian one would think most suited to work happily with the Greek. The impression left of their intercourse is friendly, and I am not sure that the Greeks of Asia Minor did so well for themselves by escaping the Persian rule. Under the Persians as under the Lydians before them, the geographic situation of the coastal cities made easy dealings with the interior a matter of large profits on both sides. Just as the Flanders wool trade has been the main thread of English history, so the great trade routes from Mesopotamia to the Aegean . . . are the threads that ever string the history of Asia Minor . . . By it the Lydians at Sardis gathered their share of the wealth of northern Asia, and transported it for western export to the cities by the sea.

The Persians, inheriting the Lydian position on the highway, also inherited the necessity of a friendly maritime people to deal with their traffic when it reached the coast. The Greek cities had the trump cards in their hands; they were repeatedly conquered, and then—because of geography—treated with care by every nation in turn that ran the Asiatic road . . . The cities of Ionia had no more to fear from Persian than from Lydian: the greater volume of trade along the highway, the stronger their own situation on the coast.

The whole Near East—not only Asia Minor—has been more populous and prosperous under an empire, whether Persian, Hellenistic, Roman, or Turkish, than when it is broken up, such as now, into many little nations, usually at each other's throat.

LIV: History Repeats Itself, but with a Twist

"The glorious fifth century B.C." was largely the result of the rising prosperity brought about by Athens's extended commercial reach. Themistocles, a leading Athenian statesman during the last Persian invasion, had convinced his fellow citizens that the road to supremacy lay not on land, but on the sea, and not by war so much as by trade. Well, isn't that Ionia's original policy—its policy for survival? And in both cases, it became the underpinnings of greatness.

Athens's commercial policy worked very well for a while, but then, like its author, its finish was dramatic. Themistocles, who had achieved the brilliant victory at Salamis, became Athens's foremost hero. He could analyze complex situations with penetrating insight and act swiftly. He was also boastful, uneducated, and not above taking bribes. He came into government service a poor man and made himself rich. He died in exile.

Under Pericles, Athens continued to follow the policy of maritime expansion, capitalizing on the transformation of Piraeus into an ample and protected port and also upon Themistocles' remission of the aliens' tax, which had brought many enterprising businessmen to Athens, stimulating commerce immensely. However, the Delian League, formed as the main vehicle of overseas expansion, became a virtual empire, breeding suspicions and animosities that led to the Peloponnesian War. That was the beginning of Athens's downfall.

LV: Let's Take a Mediterranean Cruise in the Fifth Century A.D.

If in imagination we take a merchant vessel from Naucratis to Athens, our tour of the Greek world will be complete. It was necessary that we should make this long circuit in order that we might see and feel the extent and variety of Hellenic civilization. Aristotle described the constitutional history of 158 Greek city-states, but there were a thousand more. Each contributed in commerce, industry, and thought to what we mean by Greece. In the colonies, rather than on the mainland, were born Greek poetry and prose, mathematics and metaphysics, oratory and history. Without them, and the thousand absorbing tentacles which they stretched out into the old world, Greek civilization, the most precious product in history, might never have been. Through them the cultures of Egypt and the Orient passed into Greece, and Greek culture spread slowly into Asia, Africa, and Europe.

—Will Durant,
in *The Life of Greece*

LVI: The Great Tragedians, Grandsons of Men Who Fought at Salamis and Plataea, Write Furiously and Sometimes Echo the Thunder of Zeus

How the great Athenian playwrights, who remained peerless until Shakespeare came along, were produced in this particular century can only be guessed at. Pride in how a relatively few Greeks defeated the mighty Persian Empire must be part of the answer. Another part must surely be the local body politic, composed of highly intelligent citizens who, keenly aware of life's changing fortunes, seemingly ordained by the gods, find them difficult to comprehend. Moreover, as heirs of the Renaissance that began in Ionia, they are eager for enlightenment.

Aeschylus (c. 525–456 B.C.) fought at Marathon. He wrote 70 plays, of which 7 survive.

Sophocles (d. 406 B.C.), the son of a sword manufacturer, was eighteen times the winner of first prize for his plays. Of his 113 plays, 7 survive.

Euripides (c. 484–406 B.C.) studied to be a philosopher. He wrote 75 plays; 18 survive.

LVII: Comedy Traipses Gaily Onstage, Wagging a Malicious Tongue

Epicharmus of Kos wrote about thirty-five comedies and took the new genre to Sicily, where it first took root about 484 B.C. However, it wasn't until the Peloponnesian War was under way and Aristophanes (450–380?), an aristocrat who scoffed at democracy, had his plays produced that comedy took front stage. Then its lustiness, bawdiness, and stinging ridicule of social trends seemed to fit the public's changing psychology. The low-born Cleon had come to power, following Pericles' death in 429, and was ruthlessly pursuing a commercial policy to pay for the war without raising taxes. He was able, courageous, and unscrupulous. Aristophanes ridiculed him as a false leader, ridiculed the continuing war with brother fighting brother, ridiculed, or at least ribaldly depicted onstage, the coarse manners and morals of the Athenians, with their wanton indulgence in carnal pleasures and their depravity. Comedy was a burlesque with belly laughs. It was wartime entertainment. Afterward, however, it continued to attract large audiences, for it apparently satisfied something deep in human nature.

Aristophanes wrote forty-two comedies, eleven of which survive. Some of them are still presented in major cities of the Western world. The favorites are *Lysistrata, The Frogs, The Birds*, and *The Clouds*.

Aristotle says comedy evolved from the seedtime procession where artificial phalli we carried by rollicking celebrators, disregarding the solemnity of the ancient fertility rite. Long after Aristophanes' time, comedy writers, seeking belly laughs, began to defame the heroes of the past, lampooning them, blowing up any vice they allegedly possessed. Of course they zeroed in on Sappho. It was then that she got her lurid reputation, nakedly presented, without any redeeming feature.

LVIII: Man of Action versus Man of Words

Trouble is brewing in the mountainous northeast. In Macedon, hard by Thrace, King Philip II is on the march, unifying his shepherds, farmers, and scattered nobles, welding them into the best army that Europe has seen. A handsome man with a hearty laugh and generous heart, Philip has a sure instinct for strategy, the leadership of men, and the winning tactics of battle. He loved the battlefield; he loved to carouse half the night away with his officers to celebrate a victory, and he was always victorious. Finally, he loved to find sweet respite in the arms of a beautiful woman. This can make a wife jealous.

Olympias, a tribal princess with illusions of divinity, is Philip's wife and mother of Alexander. Pella, his capital, although little more than a barbarian stronghold, is being rapidly dressed up in the splendor of marble. Macedon has no other resemblance to a city-state. Philip admires Greek culture and is determined to adopt it throughout his kingdom. Greek is the official language at court. Otherwise, its use is limited. Philip has dreams of bringing all Greek city-states under his power, by either diplomacy or force. Then, with their united strength, he will advance into Asia and crush the Persians. The time is propitious. The two strongest Greek city-states, Athens and Sparta, cannot oppose him, for they have exhausted themselves by fighting each other for twenty-seven years. Other city-states, such as Thebes, where Philip spent three studious years as a young man, are only loosely associated in a defensive league. Philip, his grandiose plan set, keeps watching for opportunities to execute its basic steps.

Demosthenes, the Athenian lawyer, statesman, and orator, perceives the menace building up in Macedon. He makes a series of passionate speeches, called the Philippics, which try to persuade the Athenians to protect their freedom. He earns the reputation as the world's greatest orator. His speeches, however, are not effective. Athenians act too late. They join with Thebes to fight Philip and are defeated. Young Alexander, commanding his father's right wing in the decisive battle, earns Philip's praise. Philip gives the vanquished generous terms and secures their goodwill. Before he can execute

196

the next step in his grand plan, however, he is murdered. He has had domestic difficulties, and Alexander wins over his father's military leaders to secure the throne.

LIX: To the Strongest . . .

When Alexander, dying in Babylon, his new capital, in 323 B.C., left his far-flung empire "to the strongest," he was speaking, he knew, realistically. That would be the inexorable way things worked out, regardless. So it came about that three of his most able generals eventually divided his huge empire among them: Antipater took over the European portion of Macedon and Greece, Seleucus fought for and finally got all of Asia, and Ptolemy got Egypt. Their hereditary kingdoms lasted for about three hundred years and provided the political framework for the Hellenistic Age.

Seleucus was the greatest monarch of his time. He ruled his polyglot kingdom from two capitals: Seleucia, a new city built on the Tigris not far from Babylon, and Antioch in Syria's Orontes valley, near the Mediterranean. His restless empire, initially reaching to Bactria and India in the east and extending from the Black Sea to the Indian Ocean, covered forty-five degrees of longitude. Rarely were all parts of it simultaneously at peace. And not always was it at peace with the kingdoms of Antipater and Ptolemy.

For the most part, though, the basic unity created by Alexander was maintained. The arteries of trade remained open and pulsed with nourishing commerce. All kinds of enterprise flourished. Greeks flocked there, seeking the promising opportunities in Sunrise Land and beyond. Great fortunes were made. Greek was the *lingua franca* of this new Magna Graecia, spoken by every ambitious person, and other aspects of Greek culture were fashionable—music, art, literature. Plays by such masters as Menander and Euripides were staged in new theaters built by prosperous cities—cities that enjoyed the Greek custom of autonomy. In a way, it seemed like a fulfillment of Alexander's envisioned Brotherhood of Man. But it was merely superficial. No fusion of peoples took place. And underneath, hidden from casual observation, the motley population was not reconciled to the Greek way of life. After all, the lower classes always outbreed the upper classes. And this majority spoke their native tongues and continued to think their racial thoughts. And as they were usually poor, miserable, and lonely, only religion could comfort them, promising them their hearts' desires, either individually or collectively.

So ancient habits of thought continued, and Eastern religions, revering ancestral ways, kept a firm grip on the diverse peoples. This was exemplified by the Jews. They rejected the Greek way of life, and when a Seleucid king tried to force it upon them they rebelled and won religious autonomy. However, there is no real distinction between Judaism and its secular state; they are theoretically one, and this led to endless difficulties. Likewise, tribal chieftains, looking back on past periods of power, tried to break out of Seleucid states and were locally successful to an increasing extent. The Seleucid Empire gradually grew smaller. For instance, the chief of an Iranian nomad tribe killed the Seleucid governor of Persia in 247 B.C. and set up the kingdom of Parthia, destined to plague the Seleucids and the Romans for centuries.

In short, the three Hellenistic kingdoms, which were absolute monarchies in accordance with self-serving Eastern traditions, did not achieve the fusion of culture and races envisioned by Alexander. Hellenism was merely the dominant medley, full of diversity, verve, excitement, and change. The tribal chant of rabbies in Jewish synagogues, then as now: "Hear, O Israel: the Lord is our God, the Lord is One," was submerged in Greek polytheism, which is inherently universal, easily perceived, modified, and adoptable by all peoples. Eventually, it, too, merged into one, helped by Greek philosophers, particularly Plato.

It was the Ptolemies, of course, not the Seleucids, who made the three Hellenistic centuries fruitful. Their promotion of Greek culture from their capital of Alexandria shaped the Western world. More specifically, it was the resident scholars at the university, such as Euclid, Eratosthenes, and Ptolemy (no relation to the royal family, so called because he was born of Greek parents in Ptolemy, a small town on the lower Nile) who had more influence on the mainland than most kings and conquerors. Eratosthenes, for example, believed the world to be a sphere and calculated its circumference at 24,662 miles (we reckon 24,847) and drew a hypothetical map thereof that prompted some daring and rewarding voyages; and Ptolemy, a meticulous compiler of celestial knowledge, published his *Almagest* (about A.D. 140), which fixed astronomical conclusions for about seventeen centuries and helped to create the science of trigonometry. He reckoned the solar year at 365¼ days minus 4 minutes and 48 seconds (an error of 6 minutes). His mean lunar month was 29 days, 12 hours, 44 minutes, and 2.5 seconds (an error of less than a second). He estimated the moon to be 250,000 miles from earth (a gross error of about 5 percent). Ptolemy's university, however, was not merely a scientific laboratory. Its august faculty, called the Alexandrines, were known primarily as the supreme literary critics, specializing in poetry. Sappho's verse must have given them endless delight.

LX: Religion, Second Phase

In conclusion, what has the religion of the Greeks to teach us that we are most in danger of forgetting? In a word, it is the faith that Truth is our friend, and that the Knowledge of Truth is not beyond our reach. Faith in honest seeking is at the heart of the Greek view of life. "Those who would rightly judge the truth," says Aristotle, "must be arbitrators, not litigants." . . . "Happy is he who has learnt the value of research," says Euripides in a fragment. Curiosity, as the Greeks knew and the Middle Ages knew not, is a virtue, not a vice. Nature, for Plato, is God's vice regent and revealer, the soul of the universe. Human nature is the same nature as the divine; no one has proclaimed this more strongly. Nature is for us; chaos and necessity are the enemy.

—W. R. Inge, D.D.,
Dean of Saint Paul's

LXI: To Steer the Right Course, Study and Reflection Are As Necessary Today As They Were Aforetime

In our schools and colleges, until quite lately, the religion of the New Testament and the traditions of the Greek and Roman classics have gone together, the one preserving us from superstition and materialism in religion, and the other making war upon the inherited barbarisms and brutalities which we have from our not very distant ancestors . . .

First comes the crude patriotism (to those ancestors) which regarded every Greek as superior to all barbarians; then came reflection, showing that not all Greeks were true bearers of the light, nor all barbarians its enemies; that Hellenism was a thing of the spirit and not dependent on the race to which a man belonged or the place where he was born . . . No people known to history formulated these ideals (Freedom, Reason, Beauty, Excellence and the pursuit of Truth) before the Greeks, and those who have spoken the words afterwards seem for the most part to be merely echoing the thoughts of old Greek men.

Those ideals . . . have been a leaven of unrest in the world. They have held up a light which is not always comforting to the eyes to see. There is another ideal which is generally stronger and may, for all we know, in the end stamp them out as evil things. There is submission instead of freedom, the deadening or brutalizing of the senses instead of Beauty, the acceptance of tradition instead of the pursuit of Truth, the belief of hallucination or passion instead of Reason and Temperate Thought, the obscurity of distinctions between good and bad and the acceptance of all human beings and all states of mind as equal in value. If something of this kind should prove in the end to be right for man, then Greece will have played the part of the great wrecker in human history. She will have held up false lights which will have lured our ship to dangerous places . . .

Whether we think these ideals the great snares of human politics, there is good cause for some of us in each generation at the cost of some time and trouble to study such important forces where they first appear consciously in the minds of our spiritual ancestors. In the thought and art of ancient Greece, more than any other, we shall find these forces, and also to some extent their great opposites, fresh, clean, and comparatively uncomplicated, with every vast issue wrought out on a small material scale and every problem stated in its lowest terms.

—Sir Gilbert Murray

LXII: Greek Civilization Began and Ended in the East

In the fourth century before Christ, the center of gravity of the Greek world began to shift eastward (after its glorious second stage centered in Athens); many Greeks emigrated to the new kingdoms of Alexander's East, and—as far as concerns Greek history—what happened in the eastern half of the Greek world mattered more than what happened in the west. In the later chapters, therefore, where our subject is the Greeks in the East, we shall find ourselves in mid-stream witnessing the culmination of Greek achievement and the final consolidation of civilizedlife . . .

The history of the Eastern Greeks still remains to be written.

Meanwhile, a touch of "fiction sometimes makes sounder history than fact."

—J. M. Cook,
in *Greeks in Ionia and the East*

. . . Still enterprising and alert, the Greeks moved by hundreds of thousands into [the new Greek kingdoms] in Asia and Egypt, Epirus and Macedon; and not only did Ionia flower again, but Hellenic blood, language and culture made its way into the interior of Asia Minor . . . across the Euphrates and the Tigris even to Bactria and India. Never had the Greek spirit shown more zest and courage; never had Greek letters and arts won so wide a victory.

—Will Durant, in *The Life of Greece*

LXIII: Epitomize Aristotle? Impossible!

Aristotle's most rewarding years may have been spent in Mytilene. There he first founded his own school, there he did most of his research in marine biology, and there he married Pythia, a native girl who gave him children and with whom he lived happily. It was from Mytilene that King Philip summoned Aristotle to tutor his headstrong son.

Aristotle's thirst for knowledge was insatiable. And his research was a tireless labor of love, including his exhaustive studies of insects and marine life.

202

Aristotle writes: "The glory, doubtless, of the heavenly bodies fills us with more delight than the contemplation of these lowly things; for the sun and stars are born not, neither do they decay, but are eternal and divine. But the heavens are high and afar off, and of celestial things the knowledge that our senses gives us is scanty and dim. The living creatures, on the other hand, are at our door, and if we so desire it we may gain ample and certain knowledge of each and all. We take pleasure in the beauty of a statue, shall not then the living fill us with delight; and all the more if in the spirit of philosophy we search for cause and recognize the evidences of design. Then will nature's purpose and her deep-seated laws be everywhere revealed, all tending in her multitudinous work to one form or another of the Beautiful."

—d'Arcy Wentworth Thompson,
in *The Legacy of Greece*

LXIV: Rome, by Adopting Greek Culture, Showed Its Greatness

"Captive Greece has taken the Roman Empire captive."

—Horace

In learning, and in every branch of literature, the Greeks are our masters.

—Cicero

A Roman boy should begin his studies with Greek, because Latin learning is derived from Greek.

—Quintilian

LXV: The First Five Roman Emperors

Augustus .... 25 B.C.–A.D. 14
Tiberius.................................. A.D. 14–37
Caligula .... A.D. 37–41
Claudius .... A.D. 41–54
Nero .... A.D. 54–68

LXVI: The Long Peace Seen through Different Eyes

Rome is the fairest of all the works of mankind, providing for people everywhere an anchorage from the wandering seas, giving to the world a stability never known before. For there now reigns among us a great peace and calm. Wars have ceased. Expulsions, seditions, tyrannies are no more—since Rome rules the world.

—Plutarch

An era of atrocities . . . Nothing but base servility and a deluge of blood shed by a despot in an hour of peace.

—Tacitus

Every street is thronged with gloomy-faced debauchees, and banquets celebrate unnatural vice and spies abound whose gentle whisper cuts men's throats.

—Juvenal

LXVII: The Augustan Age

Usually to the disgust and opposition of Augustus and Tiberius, who strongly believed in the old-fashioned virtues and the sanctity of the family, the Lesbian poets were brought to life in their regimes. This was done by three great writers who, setting a high literary standard, inaugurated the Silver

Age. Horace (65–8 B.C.), finding inspiration in the stanzas of Alcaeus, shaped his popular writings accordingly. He was much admired, and this included members of the royal households. Ovid (43 B.C. to A.D. 18) almost worshiped Sappho and built upon her amorous allusions, carrying them to extremes. He was exiled by Augustus, who also exiled his own daughter, Julia, for her notorious promiscuity. Catullus (84–54 B.C.) spent his thirty years of life in the last days of the Republic, coeval with Caesar and Cicero. His poetry, occasionally dripping with lubricity, however, was very popular in the Silver Age. Fascinated by Sappho, Catullus had named his mistress Lesbia, and the two may have been idolized by his latter-day readers. They belonged to that growing section of population that, brought to affluence by the nascent empire's prosperous times, splurged on luxury and carnal pleasures, under the aegis of fashion, and with the pretense of culture and gentility.

LXVIII: Armenia—the Buffer State

Armenia, the kingdom centered around Mount Ararat in eastern Anatolia, was used by the Romans as a buffer state against the warlike Parthians, as the latter-day Persians were called. (Tiberius put a king on the throne of Armenia as a vassal of Rome.) Eastern Anatolia, beyond the headwaters of the Euphrates, was never incorporated in the West.

However, Saint Gregory the Illuminator converted King Timidates to Christianity in A.D. 303, and it was made the official state religion before Constantine did likewise in Western Anatolia, which was part of the Roman Empire. Christianity really penetrated no farther east than Armenia. Considering Anatolia's mountainous nature, Armenia was too far inland,

and lacking an interested mouthpiece like Ionia, it didn't become part of the West. Surrounded by stronger powers and standing alone, its history was tragic.

LXIX: Pontius Pilate Asks a Question

When Pontius Pilate confronted a howling Jewish mob demanding the crucifixion of Christ, his sense of justice was outraged. The accused man deserved a fair trial, in Pilate's opinion. "Man?" came the derisive response. "He claims to be God—the Son of God." To the Jews, that was flagrant sacrilege—the worst sin, deserving death. The exact position of Pontius Pilate, the Roman proconsul of Judea, in the highly emotional episode of Jesus' crucifixion is still being debated.

The facts are unclear. Pontius Pilate was probably a good bureaucrat—the kind that keeps the empire going. He had served as proconsul in Spain before his appointment to Judea, then a troublesome part of Rome's province of Syria. And he was of equestrian rank—a Roman aristocrat of independent means—which means he was less likely to take graft and a man of some culture. In any case, his job was to keep the Roman peace in Palestine, and he reported directly to Tiberius. And out of the welter of conflicting reports regarding the crucifixion, out of the tumultuous emotions frozen into unyielding positions, one thing stands out: when someone testified that he had come "to bear witness to the truth," Pilate wearily asked, "What is truth?" And that forlorn query has echoed down through the ages, without a satisfactory reply.

LXX: The Apocalypse (What Is Hidden) Becomes Revelations

On Patmos, an Ionian isle about twelve miles from Ephesus, the last book of the New Testament was written. Dedicated to the Seven Churches of Asia—Ephesus, Smyrna, Pergamos, Thyatira, Sardis, Philadelphia, and Laodicea—it was written by John of Ephesus, who may have been John, son of Zebedee, who was one of Christ's first disciples and after the resurrection worked with Peter in Jerusalem. In Ephesus, where he had sought refuge with other early Christians, he was banished to Patmos, possibly during an anti-Christian persecution. There is no doubt, however, about the inspiration that enabled him to evoke awe and emulation down through the ages. Like Saint Paul, he was a master of Greek language, and never have the poetic riches of that tongue, and its seemingly inherent dedication to truth, been better displayed. Few books of the Bible have contributed more phrases to general English usage: "Be thou faithful unto death, and I will give thee a crown of life" (2:10); "He shall rule them with a rod of iron" (2:27); "I know thy works, thou art neither cold nor hot" (3:15, words addressed to the church in Laodicea); "I am Alpha and Omega, the beginning and the end, the first and the last" (22:14). Even so, much of Revelations is beyond the reach of words and is told in symbols: seven continually recurs as a significant number, four beasts praise God, four seals are broken, and four horsemen ride forth, the last of which is mounted on a pale horse and symbolizes death.

As the prophecies of pestilence, earthquake, and warfare fade, the vision of the reward awaiting the faithful in heaven becomes brighter: "And the angel carried me away in spirit to a great and high mountain, and showed me that great city, the holy Jerusalem, descending out of heaven from God, having the glory of God: and her light was like unto a stone most precious, even like a jasper stone, clear as crystal" (21:10–11).

The woman, Babylon, is believed to mean Rome, the city on the seven hills, and the five kings who have already fallen can only mean Augustus, Tiberius, Caligula, Claudius, and Nero. The persecution referred to would be that under Nero, and the author's main purpose may be to encourage Christians to have faith, for the Kingdom of God is at hand. Indeed, no passage has brought more comfort to the dying and the bereaved through every subsequent age than Revelation 21:4–5: "God shall wipe away all tears from their eyes: and there shall be no more death, neither sorrow, nor crying, neither shall there be any more pain; for the former things are passed away. And he that sat on the throne said, Behold I make all things new."

LXXI: "That Which Hath Been Is That Which Shall Be"

Those famous words by Thucydides are drumbeats to EC's long march, replicating the mighty Roman Empire, stretching from Briton to the Near East, creating a continental common market to foster prosperity in all member nations.

Economic well-being! That's the policy Ionia pursued to build its greatness?

LXXII: Brush Up on Latin? No Kidding?

Well, it might come in handy a long way down the pike. Latin may eventually become the EC's common language. It worked before. And that precedent may become an irresistible goal.

Of course the EC may not be able to achieve its dream. That's a drama we can watch unfold over the next decade.

LXXIII: Let's Put a Colophon to It

Colophon's famed cavalry regiment, a notoriously swank riding club in peacetime, always managed to snatch victory in every war in which it participated, proudly spawning the popular phrase: Let's put a colophon to it.

LXXIV: And Now Good-bye

As an envoi, let's join in singing Homer's "Hymn to Apollo." The hymn is believed to have been written a long time after the Poet's death by an unknown bard, which shows Homer's grip on the public imagination.

> Well, may Apollo keep you all! and so,
> Sweethearts, goodbye—yet tell me not to go
> Out from your hearts; as if in after hours
> Some other wanderer in this world of ours
> Touch at your shores, and ask your maidens here
> Who sings the songs the sweetest to your ear,
> Think of me then, and answer with a smile,
> A blind old man of Scio's rocky isle.

End.